SLAYING CHICAGO

Curated by Leigh M. Clark

Aurora Corialis Publishing

Pittsburgh, PA

OTHER COLLECTIVES BY LEIGH M. CLARK

Slaying Southwest Florida

Slaying Tampa Bay

Slaying Atlanta

Slaying Nashville

Slaying Sarasota

Slaying Boston

Slaying Las Vegas

The Dream is in Your Hands

The Dream is in Your Hands: She Can Do It

Living Kindly: Bold Conversations About the Power of
Kindness

Table of Contents

Introduction: Chicago, the City That Slayed My Heart

Leigh M. Clark

I didn't choose Chicago. In 1994, my parents made that choice for me. I was pulled from Long Island—ripped from the place I knew best, where my childhood memories were rooted in the constant hum of New York energy. I was a New York girl through and through. I had my friends, my school, and even my shining moment as the very blonde Maria in my junior high's production of West Side Story. I felt like I was on my way. But then came Chicago—specifically, its suburbs—and I wasn't ready.

I didn't want to leave the city that had raised me. I didn't want to trade the buzz of New York for the quiet of the Midwest. But I learned something quickly: Chicago doesn't ask you if you're ready. It just happens to you.

The City That Crept In

It started with the small things. The simple joys of high school, driving with friends through stretches of developing subdivisions where cornfields kissed the horizon. Windows down, music up, feeling like we had the whole world in front of us. And yet, it was the city that called to me most.

I learned how easy it was to find my way downtown, to cut class for a show or to quietly escape a field trip to The Art Institute and make my own path. I remember the sheet of paper folded in my pocket—handwritten recommendations from my New York friends who had already ventured to Chicago. Go here. Try this. Don't miss that. I was following a roadmap of someone else's memories, but somewhere along the way, I started creating my own.

I discovered Belmont and Clark. I wandered into the shops, sat in cafes, and watched the pulse of the city beat in time with my curiosity. Chicago wasn't trying to be New York. It didn't have to. It was raw and honest and completely unapologetic. It was a city that didn't ask for permission, and that matched the stubborn streak I carried with me.

And as much as I hated to admit it, I was falling in love.

Chicago: A City Built by Bold Women

Chicago is a city that thrives because of the boldness and brilliance of its women. It's a place where ideas come to life, where women rise and create legacies that shape industries, communities, and culture. Today, women make up more than 51% of Chicago's population, and they are the backbone of its progress.

Nearly 36.5% of new venture-backed companies in Chicago have at least one woman founder—one of the highest rates in the nation. (chicagoblend.org) These women are redefining what success looks like, creating businesses that drive innovation and foster community. More than 457,000 women-owned businesses call Illinois home, contributing significantly to the state's economy. (gov.illinois.gov)

But it's not just about business. Chicago women are artists, entrepreneurs, educators, and leaders. They are reshaping neighborhoods, creating spaces for culture, and nurturing the next generation of change-makers.

This city is built on resilience, and that resilience is reflected in every woman who has faced challenges, stood her ground, and built something lasting. It's in the women who support each other, who collaborate instead of compete, and who are determined to leave their mark.

Because in Chicago, women know that rising together is the only way to rise at all.

Etching My Own Chicago Memories

It wasn't long before Chicago's traditions became mine. Christmas Eve dinners at the Fairmont, where the city glowed under winter's chill, became a family ritual. The reflections of twinkling lights on the river, the hush of the streets dusted with snow—those moments rooted Chicago deeper into my story.

I think about standing outside that daisy wheel parking garage, posing for photos, feeling like I was part of something bigger than I could understand at the time. I think about crashing a float at the St. Patrick's Day parade, pulled up by my drunk Uncle Jack who thought it was a great idea to just hop on. We weren't invited, but Chicago didn't care. They let us throw candy anyway. Because Chicago is the kind of place where, if you show up, you're welcome.

I remember the acts of kindness I performed at the Bean years later. I stood there, not as a visitor, but as someone who wanted to give something back. Chicago had given me so much, and it felt right to return even just a fraction of that goodness.

And now, it's the memories I'm building with my son that matter most. I've shown him the same paths I once wandered. The feeling of running free in the fields of DeKalb. The magic of riding the Ferris wheel at Navy Pier, the city stretching out beneath us. I wanted him to know Chicago—not just its landmarks but its stories. Its heartbeat.

The Women Who Define This Book

Slaying Chicago is a tribute to the women who are creating the city's legacy, one bold step at a time. The women in this book are innovators, leaders, artists, and creators. They are women who have fought for their dreams and made them real. They are women who didn't wait for a seat at the table—they built the table themselves.

And more than anything, they are women who know the power of lifting others as they rise.

This is a city where women support each other. Where they collaborate, create, and connect. The women in *Slaying Chicago* reflect the very best of what the city stands for: resilience, grit, kindness, and the courage to dream big.

Each story is a testament to what's possible when determination meets opportunity. These women show us that leadership isn't about doing it alone—it's about reaching back and pulling someone up with you. It's about knowing that success is even sweeter when it's shared.

Slaying Chicago

That's what *Slaying Chicago* is about.

This book, the sixth in the Slay the USA series, isn't just a collection of stories—it's a celebration of women who have carved their place in this city, who have fought for their dreams, and who have learned that collaboration is the most powerful form of leadership.

These women didn't wait for permission. They showed up. They created. They took risks. And they wrote their stories on the skyline.

Chicago taught me to do the same.

It's where I learned that resilience isn't about being tough for toughness' sake. It's about knowing that you can fall, you can fail, and you can get back up stronger. It's about learning that failure isn't the end, but part of the blueprint.

I am so proud of this book. I am proud of the women in these pages and the paths they've forged. I am proud of this city, for the way it shapes us and for the way it lets us shape it right back.

Because Chicago doesn't just give you memories. It gives you purpose.

Chicago slayed my heart. I know it will slay yours too.

The Beautiful Garden of Life:

Why Planting Seeds of Kindness

Produces Lifelong Blooms

Kathleen Sarpy

For more than 30 years, Kathleen Sarpy has enjoyed a diverse career in public relations and marketing, working with the world's most recognizable brands and corporations, and also serving as the driving force behind emerging start-ups and charities. With unrivaled energy and enthusiasm, Kathleen expertly connects people, events and ideas to generate meaningful and lasting impact. A former senior executive at a leading global PR firm, Kathleen left her "big agency" life behind in January 2001 after the birth of her first child to bootstrap her own firm without a solid backup plan. Alone in her suburban basement, seven months pregnant with her second child and only armed with a laptop, tons of tenacity, and goodwill, Kathleen's goal was simple: Offer world-class strategy and unbridled creativity to the world's most respected companies by eliminating bureaucracy—without sacrificing kindness or her focus on motherhood.

Now more than twenty-four years later, Kathleen manages an incredibly talented team of professionals that supports dozens of global, national, and Chicago-based clients in the consumer packaged goods, hospitality, finance, real estate, and nonprofit spaces.

Kathleen has never lost sight of the "5" in her value-driven company's name that remains the cornerstone of her business: kindness, creativity, passion, hustle, and integrity. Throughout its evolution, Agency H5 has been recognized alongside the best PR firms in the world, having won numerous awards and recognition over the years.

Beyond her professional commitments, Kathleen finds deep value in giving back through mentorship and empowering future generations of female leaders. She also proudly supports a number of civic organizations and local philanthropies that reflect her dedication to Chicagoland including Girl Scouts, Ronald McDonald House Charities and CC's Wishlist among others. A proud Distinguished Alumni and Phi Beta Kappa graduate of Purdue University (class of 1992), she founded the Purdue Women's Network in 2017 to unite, motivate, engage, and inspire 200,000 alumni worldwide. She also was proud to be inducted into the 2024 class of Purdue Old Masters which recognized her commitment to mentorship.

If you ask her, though, her biggest and proudest achievement to date is being a mother of six incredible children ages twenty-five to sixteen. She resides in Wheaton, Ill., with her husband Chris and one uncooperative English bulldog named Hope.

You can follow her @kathleensarpy.

For as long as I can remember, I have seen my life as one big, exquisite garden filled with the people I've encountered throughout my experiences. Since I was a small child running through the oversized lilac bushes that surrounded my suburban backyard, I've loved being around lush greens and flowers. Their sweet fragrance and bright colors always brought me an overwhelming sense of tranquility, joy, and happiness. I recall becoming giddy when I received flowers from thoughtful friends and loved ones who knew how much blooms brighten my world. In my adult life, I began my own tradition of grabbing simple bouquets at my suburban French market each weekend to place in vases around my home and add vibrancy to my office. That simple ritual continues to bring me peace, and is a constant reminder that witnessing the world's natural beauty is a true gift.

I've always been a nurturer and someone who derives great pleasure from helping people grow and flourish—much like a gardener tends to the beautiful flowers in a summer garden. Mentorship and the championing of other women have been two areas that have deeply enriched my career and added a special element of meaning to my life's profession in public relations and marketing. Yet, my very first opportunity to tend to one my life's "gardens" was through the birth of my five children and the joy of parenting a total of six kids (through a happy remarriage).

In the early '90s, I graduated from Purdue University in less than three years. I then catapulted up the ranks at some of the world's most regarded public relations firms at a rather young age. At twenty-eight, I hit my first major "crossroads of conscience" after the birth of my first child, Emily. While I loved both my job and my rapidly expanding family, I quickly became aware that my priorities had become forever inversed. When I learned that I was pregnant with my second child, a son, I knew I had to focus on tending to my family first, realizing that a "big agency" job was not conducive to my fierce commitment to motherhood. So as a new mother with two babies under sixteen months of age, I launched my own public relations firm, which I built from the ground up. All I had was my modest suburban basement, a laptop, an old-school Rolodex, and a good dose of humility and tenacity. I got to work connecting with and helping as many people as I could to grow and nurture my fledgling firm.

I watered and tended to my nascent business, and after months of worry and self-doubt, Agency H5 began to grow and flourish; I took on blue-chip global clients that were seeking global agency thinking and talent without the bureaucracy or bloated budgets of the big firms. Now nearly twenty-five years later, that little basement business has grown into an award-winning, nationally recognized agency based in Chicago that keeps the big global firms on their toes.

Through the early days of my company's growth, I was simultaneously raising a crop (literally!) of children that were all born within the first decade of my company's existence. Emily, John Henry, Haley, Brady, and Finley were my highest priority to tend to every day. The deep joy and satisfaction I gained from nurturing, loving, and watching them grow into the beautiful and unique people they are now cannot be easily measured. Today, they navigate life with grace and kindness and have already experienced an early lesson about the value of resilience during life's many storms.

Throughout my fifty-three years on this earth, the hundreds—more likely thousands—of my friendships and business relationships have been rooted in planting intentional seeds of love, kindness, and goodwill. I genuinely love the ability to meet someone, formulate a deep and authentic connection, and support or serve them in some way; it's just how I'm wired. It's also perhaps why I excel in the communications-forward field of public relations and marketing. I regularly marvel at, and am truly humbled by, what has bloomed in this gorgeous "life garden" of mine.

As I move through seasons of change—marriage, motherhood, love, loss—I constantly find myself in awe of how those simple "seeds" have grown and sprouted at just the right time, offering color, joy, comfort, or tranquility when I needed it most. Work challenges, deception, an unexpected divorce after eighteen years of marriage, and the devastating loss of both of my parents within fourteen weeks of each other, brought some of my darkest days— and those interpersonal blooms sustained me and offered hope. We all experience dark days, and relationships provide deep beauty and personal growth, just like flowers do.

My family will tell you that I am definitely NOT a gardener, but I am familiar with the terms "annual" and "perennial"; annuals are plants that pop out for just one season, and you get to enjoy all of their splendor. On the other hand, perennials live for three or often more growing seasons, ready for nurturing and pruning to be passed on, even for generations. In my relationship garden, many flowers have bloomed for a long time, and they've continually reminded me of the joy they bring and how fortunate I am to know them and love them. Other people I've met were annuals, which makes them no less beautiful or appreciated. These timely blooms gave me beauty or a blessing for one important season in my life—to teach me something, connect me to someone I needed for my next chapter, or create a bridge to a bigger garden in my future. So, although these gorgeous blooms may not return next season, I'm grateful I could appreciate them for the moment.

After suffering from the losses of life, I gave myself permission to also prune the "weeds" of my garden—those personal or professional relationships that don't provide beauty or instead take up valuable space for other new flowers to grow and flourish. In my past, I was often hesitant to remove those weeds, perhaps due to family ties, a sense of loyalty, or a desire to hold onto the past in some way. However, through life and experiences, I have realized that it is okay to do this exercise to ensure my life is fertile for new relationships to grow. And grow they have.

Nearly twenty-five years after starting my company, Agency H5—which was founded on the five core principles and values of kindness, creativity, passion, hustle, and integrity—I have been fortunate to tend to and nurture the professional growth of hundreds of employees, most of whom women in similar early-career situations to myself with growing families and opportunities. I have grown immensely from the experience of "watering" and tending to these relationships as I deeply value the women who have been vulnerable with me in sharing their own stories and mentoring me along my own professional and personal journey. We all have friends who help us grow and flourish, and mine are a group I consistently count on to bring color and texture to my life.

To further tend to and better enjoy the "gardens" in your own life, consider reflecting on the following rules of relationship "gardening:"

- You DO reap what you sow. Plant seeds with intention and abundance, throwing goodness wherever it might take root. Please note that all sprouts do not bloom immediately or simultaneously. The blessings of those seeds will bloom over time and right when you need them most. I continue to marvel at this lesson as I navigate the ups and downs of life.
- Don't judge a bloom at first blush. Often beautiful friendships can blossom from unexpected places. As we age, we often settle into our comfortable habits and, as a result, our world may become a bit smaller as a result. Find ways to expand your life for new relationships to take root and keep open to those that are annuals or perennials.
- Weeds that are green or lush will never be a flower. Don't be afraid to uproot unhealthy, weedy relationships from your garden to ensure your soil is ready for new plantings and growth. We only have so much time, energy, and

space in our lives for people or things that don't bring us joy.

- Be a bee in the world. Help pollinate the "life gardens" of your friends and loved ones through sharing your wisdom, learnings, and lessons. I've always been a big believer of making strategic connections between two women I admire and then getting out of the way to allow new roots of friendship to form.
- Never forget to water and nurture your own garden. If you're emotionally arid or living on salted earth, it will be impossible for others to thrive in your life. You must find the sunshine, bask in the rain and know that growth occurs when you're taking care of you.

In each season of springtime when the world begins to bloom outdoors, I always feel a wonderful sense of optimism and excitement for what beauty will be revealed in the upcoming year. I'm also reminded how grateful I am for the beautiful garden of people in my life. I encourage you to intentionally plant seeds of love and kindness, too. It will yield countless colorful experiences and a beautiful haven to weather the various seasons of your life.

Grills, Grazing and Going for it:

My Leap from Finance to Food

Babs

After a successful 25-year corporate career, Babs followed her lifelong passion for entertaining and founded Babs Boards in 2021. Her expertise in charcuterie and hospitality quickly earned her recognition as a go-to entertaining expert. She has taught over 150 Charcuterie & Girls Who Grill classes, designed stunning custom grazing tables for a variety of events, and mentored aspiring culinary talents. Her career highlights include appearances on WGN, Fox, and CBS, as well as leading a charcuterie class at the iconic Wrigley Field. In 2025, Babs expanded her offerings with the launch of Babs Entertains, where she continues to inspire and teach others how to host unforgettable gatherings in their own homes.

Instagram: @babsboards

https://www.facebook.com/babsboards1/

https://www.linkedin.com/in/alison-beitzel-8a09b7335

As a child, I was not a foodie. Whether it was my pickiness or my mom's cooking (no offense, Mom), the debate still lingers. I was also mostly a vegetarian for many years—which makes me laugh now, considering how much I love meat. I didn't even eat Thanksgiving turkey, and I used to put A1 sauce on everything. Back in the '80s in a suburb of Cleveland, Ohio, we didn't have many options outside of bland, overcooked meals. My very first memory of being excited about anything food-related was my dad's "hot sauce," or what we now know as spicy salsa. Back then, international foods were not prevalent at all, and the only Mexican food we could get was Chi-Chis, which my parents didn't EVER go to because my dad didn't like cheese, also humorous considering I am now the (self-proclaimed) charcuterie queen. So when my Dad made "hot sauce" I was awakened to a whole new world. There was only one type of tortilla chips to buy, round Tostitos, and I dipped these into the "hot sauce" and was immediately in love.

My parents are still avid entertainers who host amazing dinner parties, and have been doing this for as long as I can remember. They joke that I'm such a great sleeper because I used to sleep during their dinners with friends which became inevitable late-night dance parties. I learned at an early age that they definitely had fun at their own party—an adage I teach everyone in my classes now. I don't remember them being amazing cooks growing up, and they really did not teach me much about cooking. For them, dinner parties were less about the food and more about the connection with friends.

In college, my taste buds were in for a shock when a good friend recommended a Thai restaurant. We only had a few Chinese restaurants in Ohio and I never heard of a Thai restaurant. My boyfriend pronounced it "thigh" food, because we were totally clueless about ethnic cuisine, and we went to give it a try... and wow, the spices and flavors were absolutely out of this world! No A1 sauce needed. At that moment, I learned there was a whole world out there with amazing flavors and spices, and I wanted to discover it all. That boyfriend did not last, but my appreciation for Thai food did, and it's still my favorite cuisine.

In my sophomore year of college, we went to Cancun for spring break. This was my first time out of the country, and my friends ordered guacamole. I didn't think I liked avocados. My parents didn't, so I must not either, right? Wrong. They convinced me to try the chips and guacamole, and I started to realize that maybe fresh, local foods were the best way to really enjoy food. (Of course, the margaritas helped too.)

I backpacked around Europe for two months after college with my boyfriend, Matt, who later became my husband. That is when I discovered the most amazing foods all over Europe and officially became a foodie. We were on a strict $50/ day budget, including lodging, so that meant fresh bread, cheese, olives, and sangria in Spain, warm chocolate croissants in Paris, and gelato for all three meals in Italy. Eating well did not mean Michelin-star restaurants—it meant fresh, high-quality, and local specialties. This realization became the foundation of how I approach entertaining and cooking today. I got the travel bug that trip; I don't know if it was Matt, the beautiful countries, the food and drinks, or all of the above, but I could not wait to save money to take more trips to Europe. (I never had A1 sauce again.)

I started my career in audit at KPMG in Chicago, Ill., and quickly realized that I wasn't passionate about accounting—I was just chasing the money. I didn't cook, mostly because the hours were long and I ate dinner at work, but also because I didn't know how to cook anything aside from mac and cheese. One night, as I ate yet another bowl of cereal for dinner, Matt raised an eyebrow. "When we have kids, you can't serve them this for dinner every night," he said.

He was right; I needed to learn to cook.

We were lucky to live in a city with so many wonderful restaurants, and enjoyed trying new ones in our neighborhood. We went to Charlie Trotters and did the full wine pairings before we even had any idea what haute cuisine was or why wine pairings are a bad idea (just the headache afterwards is the bad part). Matt stayed in New York City from time to time, and I had the pleasure of joining him on numerous occasions. This small-town-Ohio girl was absolutely mesmerized by Manhattan's restaurants, diners, coffee shops, and bars. My friend toured me around Dean & Deluca, a specialty grocery store in SoHo, and I was introduced to many foods I didn't even know existed, let alone in one place. I also realized I had access to all kinds of amazing European foods much closer to home. We traveled to Europe a few more times, and each time, I loved the travel (and the food) even more.

Our children Max and Emerson were born in 2004 and 2005; by then, I was very motivated to prove Matt wrong—I was going to learn to cook. A few life-changing events helped me feed my kids something other than cereal every night. My friend bought me the very first *Barefoot Contessa* cookbook by Ina Garten. I read it cover to cover and really loved the message, which reminded me of my European travels. First, you don't need a million steps or ingredients or complicated recipes to make a wonderful meal; second, buy fresh, in-season, high-quality ingredients. Following these rules makes all the difference in the world.

Another good friend was really getting into cooking and was teaching me what she had learned in my own kitchen. She worked with Chicago culinary icons Gale Gand, Charlie Trotter, and Grant Achatz, and she taught cooking classes at a local cooking school, but I got free classes in her personal kitchen. She even gave me some of the recipes for dishes sold at these famous restaurants to try at home. (Don't tell them I said that!)

Good friends of ours, Robin and Sean, would have us over for dinner every chance possible. We cooked together while our young kids played, and we experimented with recipes from new cookbooks with new flavors ... and lots of wine. Sean and I would trash the kitchen, and Robin would clean it. We ate like kings (or at least our thirtysomething selves thought so).

Matt was working and traveling a lot, and I wanted to learn how to grill so I didn't need him for a grilled meal. I took grilling classes at a local seafood store and learned a lot—but it wasn't until I had girlfriends over for dinner that I was forced to use my grilling skills. That day, Matt was supposed to be home in time to grill for us, but he unexpectedly had to work late. I didn't want to let on that my dinner was going to be ruined if I didn't grill properly. So I turned the grill on and prayed my skills for seafood applied to chicken. My friends were none the wiser, the chicken was perfect, and I officially became a "Girl who Grills" in that moment.

And I did not feed my kids cereal for dinner.

In 2021, I retired from the corporate world after a twenty-five-year career in accounting and finance. I wanted to find something fun to do, and I knew it wouldn't be accounting. One weekend in Texas, after several glasses of wine and laughs, Robin came up with a wild idea I hadn't considered: "Babs, you should start a charcuterie business in Chicago. You'd be perfect for it." Remembering our days cooking and having many dinner parties together, she thought a charcuterie business would be a perfect fit. Although it sounded crazy at the time, it really felt like a natural extension of everything I loved: making great food, creating something beautiful, and most importantly, bringing people together.

Robin has always called me "Babs"; I'm not sure she knows my real name is "Alison." "Babs" is a derivation from my maiden name, "Barr," which became "Barbie" in college and morphed into "Babs." With our teenage daughters listening in, I decided to take the leap and start a charcuterie business. But what was I going to call it? Robin said, "Well, Babs, you are going to call it 'Babs Boards' of course." Of course. Her daughter hand-drew my logo. So special.

I thought my new venture was going to be something part-time, just something I could do for friends. Matt thought I was absolutely crazy and wasn't sure that I would make any money. We were both wrong—wow, did it grow quickly through the power of social media! Babs Boards began as a fun thing to fill my time during retirement, but quickly grew into a profitable business. It started with charcuterie boards, but expanded into dessert, veggies, breakfast boards, and grazing tables.

I love charcuterie boards, mostly because I love cheese, but really because they exemplify everything I learned from my parents about entertaining: have fun at your own party! The way they taught me to have fun is to make sure you have everything you possibly can have done in advance before your guests arrive. *Everything.* That way, you can really spend time with your guests and connect through conversation. Isn't that what dinner parties are all about?

I never thought I could have so much fun creating displays of food on kitchen islands and dining room tables, but I did it—for countless graduation parties, birthdays, showers, and just about any kind of gathering imaginable. Talk about the opposite of debits and credits! Someone recently asked me if I was a bad accountant because my new business seemed like a major pivot from the finance world; I told them you can see my accounting background in the organization and perfect lines on each of my grazing tables.

I sold my charcuterie-board-making part of the business to our local butcher shop, and continued to design grazing tables. But a life-changing moment came in early 2022, when a customer asked if I taught charcuterie classes. I had never taught anything in my life before, but I wanted to give it a try! My mom is a retired first-grade teacher, so it must be in our genes. I said "yes," and did a trial run with my friends. My first paid class was for fifty women with a grazing table too. My friend helped with the class, and I will never forget sharing a bottle of wine afterward and toasting to our accomplishment. I came home that evening utterly exhausted, but with the biggest smile on my face. I'd found my passion! I really didn't know if I would ever be hired to teach a charcuterie class again, but I sure hoped I would.

Turns out it was the perfect timing for my charcuterie classes to be wildly successful. In early 2022, people began gathering in person again, and the pent-up demand for connection was instrumental to my success. The charcuterie craze was in full-force, and everyone wanted to learn how to make a salami rose. Moms who hadn't been out much since before COVID were eager to have a night away from kid duty and have fun with their friends. And I was absolutely loving every second of it. I felt a bit like a Tupperware saleswoman packing up my car with charcuterie items and driving all around town to teach.

Although I had several people take my charcuterie class more than once (I like to think that I was such a great teacher that they kept coming back for more—but they really just wanted another "Mom's night out"), I was looking for new class ideas. So I launched "Girls Who Grill" and decided to make that class part of my offerings.

I continue to reinvent and expand. Instead of Babs Boards, it is now Babs Entertains. (It's still Babs Boards too, but a whole lot more!) Whether I'm helping someone host unforgettable gatherings, teaching people how to master the grill, or creating new ways to make entertaining easy and fun, I want to help through teaching and sharing.

I'm so incredibly thankful that I have an amazing husband and so many friends who believed in me and supported me from day one. I jumped feet first into entrepreneurship, which I knew nothing about. I said "yes" to everything at the beginning until I found my true passion—teaching. My parents instilled in me the confidence to step out of my comfort zone, trust myself and to take risks. The funny thing is that I never wanted to be a teacher when I was younger, because I was always following the money. It's not lost on me that my Mom, the retired teacher, may have not taught me a thing about cooking, but she actually taught me the most.

From Humble Beginnings to Empowering Beauty

Diana Diaz

Diana Diaz, MSN, APRN, FNP-C, is a dedicated family nurse practitioner and the visionary founder of DEMI Med Spa, located in Chicago, Ill. With over a decade of nursing experience, Diana seamlessly transitioned from oncology care to aesthetic medicine, embodying her commitment to holistic wellness and patient-centered care.

Born and raised in Rosenberg, Texas, Diana's journey is a testament to resilience and determination. Overcoming personal challenges, including becoming a mother at a young age, she pursued her passion for healthcare with unwavering dedication. After earning her nursing degree from Houston Baptist University in 2009, Diana began her career in oncology, providing empathetic care to patients facing critical health challenges. In 2018, she expanded her expertise into aesthetic medicine, combining her clinical skills with an artistic eye to help clients enhance their natural beauty.

At DEMI Med Spa, Diana specializes in advanced aesthetic injectables, including fillers, neuromodulators, and regenerative treatments like Platelet-Rich Fibrin (PRF). Her holistic approach focuses not just on aesthetics but also on overall well-being, ensuring clients feel comfortable and confident throughout the process. Diana's commitment to continuous education keeps her at the forefront of the latest techniques and products in the aesthetic industry.

Fluent in both English and Spanish, Diana is dedicated to making aesthetic services accessible to a diverse clientele. Her compassionate demeanor and meticulous attention to detail have earned her a loyal following and numerous positive testimonials. Through DEMI Med Spa, Diana continues to empower individuals, helping them feel confident and radiant in their own skin.

www.demimedspa.com

In the heart of Chicago's vibrant aesthetic scene, I stand as a testament to resilience and empowerment. As the founder of DEMI Med Spa, my journey from humble beginnings in Rosenberg, Texas, to becoming a renowned aesthetic nurse practitioner reflects my unwavering determination and passion for holistic wellness.

My story begins in Rosenberg, a small town where opportunities were limited, but community and family bonds were strong. Growing up in a modest one bedroom home shared with my parents and three siblings, I learned early on the values of hard work, perseverance, and gratitude. The living room often doubled as a bedroom, a testament to our family's resourcefulness and unity. Despite financial constraints, my parents instilled in us the importance of education, believing it to be the key to a better future.

Life took an unexpected turn when I became pregnant at sixteen. Facing societal stereotypes and statistical odds stacked against young Hispanic mothers from low-income backgrounds, I refused to let my circumstances define my future. With unwavering determination, I balanced the challenges of motherhood with my educational aspirations. Walking across the stage to receive my high school diploma with my five-month-old daughter in my arms symbolized my resilience and commitment to forging a better path.

Inspired by my daughter's grandmother, Marcy, a compassionate neonatal nurse, I found my calling in healthcare. I enrolled at Houston Baptist University, where I juggled the demands of nursing school and motherhood. Graduating in 2009, I embarked on my nursing career, initially focusing on oncology. My experiences in oncology deepened my empathy and reinforced my commitment to patient-centered care.

After years in oncology, I sought to expand my impact on patient wellness. Recognizing the profound connection between self-perception and overall health, I transitioned into aesthetic medicine in 2018. This move allowed me to blend my clinical skills with an artistic touch, helping clients enhance their natural beauty while promoting holistic well-being.

In 2023, I founded DEMI Med Spa in Chicago, a sanctuary for medicine, aesthetics, and wellness. My vision was to create a space where clients feel empowered, confident, and cared for. Each treatment at DEMI is tailored to the individual's unique features and goals, ensuring personalized and natural results. My holistic approach emphasizes not just the aesthetic outcome but also the client's overall well-being, reflecting my belief that true beauty emanates from within.

My dedication to excellence is evident in my commitment to ongoing education. I actively seek advanced training and stay abreast of the latest techniques and products in the aesthetic industry. This dedication ensures that my clients receive the highest standard of care and the most innovative treatments available.

Beyond my clinical practice, I am passionate about empowering others, particularly minority women facing similar challenges. By sharing my journey, I hope to inspire others to pursue their dreams, regardless of their starting point. My story is a powerful reminder that with determination, resilience, and self-belief, anything is possible.

My journey from a young mother facing adversity to a successful entrepreneur and healthcare provider exemplifies strength and perseverance. Through DEMI Med Spa, I continue to make a lasting impact, one that extends beyond aesthetics into the hearts of those who witness my inspiring story.

Resilience in Motion: the Art of Starting Over

Loli DiSanto

Loli is a full-time artist, celebrated for creating dazzling, three-dimensional sculptures that bring joy and inspiration to homes. With collections featured in galleries across the United States, her art combines bold colors, intricate craftsmanship, and a signature "touch" of sparkle. But beyond the color and crystal-encrusted details lies a deeper purpose: Loli wants to be remembered as someone who truly sparkles from within.

Born and raised in Chicago, Loli spent her early years as a competitive figure skater, which first ignited her love for all things luminous. After earning a degree in physiology from Michigan State University and graduating from Midwestern University as a physician assistant, she discovered her passion for art later in life. She immersed herself in art education through workshops, private lessons, and a journey of creative exploration.

In addition to her artistic pursuits, Loli has been deeply committed to community engagement, having served on the Women's Board at the Adler Planetarium, the Lurie Children's Service Board, and the Alliance for Early Childhood Development Board.

Her work, often described as "jewelry for the home" reflects her belief that beauty on the outside should resonate with the light within. While the sparkle of her sculptures captures the eye, Loli hopes her legacy will shine through the impact she has on others. She inspires those around her to dream boldly, embrace creativity, and cultivate an inner brilliance that matches the radiance they share with the world. In her words, "Always remember to SPARKLE!" You can sparkle on the outside all you want, but what truly matters is the beautiful person who shines from within.

www.lolidisanto.com

@loli_disanto_artist

Growing up in Chicago, I was immersed in the sparkling world of figure skating—a sport that was as beautiful as it was brutal. From the age of four through college, my days were spent in skating rinks, training relentlessly for hours, pushing my body to its limits. On the ice, there was elegance and grace; off the ice, there was discipline, drive, and a steady stream of bruises and sore muscles. Learning new jumps was a constant cycle of leaping, falling, and then getting back up, again and again, thousands of times. Each failed attempt was painful and discouraging, but it also taught me resilience. I learned that every fall, no matter how hard, was just a step toward mastering the next jump. Each time I got back up, I felt a little stronger, a little more determined, and a little closer to my goal.

I carried this fierce, unyielding spirit with me beyond the rink, and it became part of who I was. When I started my undergraduate studies in physiology at Michigan State University's Lyman Briggs School, it was clear that many of my peers struggled with the long hours and rigorous coursework. For me, the grueling training in figure skating had prepared me for this. School wasn't easy—it tested my endurance, required focus, and often felt like an uphill battle. But every late-night study session, every challenging exam, reminded me of my training on the ice. If I could fall a thousand times on the rink and still get up, then I could conquer whatever challenges my academic journey threw my way.

My family was my strongest support system during these years. My dad, who had always encouraged me to keep going no matter what, was a constant source of motivation. With his calming voice and simple wisdom, he would tell me to "keep trucking." Every time I faced a setback or a moment of self-doubt, he reminded me that perseverance was key and that true success wasn't in never failing but in always getting back up. He believed in me, and that belief gave me a confidence I carried forward.

When I graduated and became a physician assistant, I was ready to commit myself to helping others. For years, I worked in healthcare, driven by a desire to make a difference. But over time, my life took an unexpected turn. I felt a tug in a different direction, a quiet call toward art. At first, it was a whisper of curiosity, a hobby I explored in my free time. But as I immersed myself in painting, sculpture, and the world of visual art, that whisper grew louder. The same passion I'd once felt on the ice and in my medical career was surfacing, but in a new way.

Choosing to leave medicine and embrace art full-time was a huge leap of faith. There was a voice of doubt, one that questioned whether I was giving up something stable for something uncertain. But every time I felt hesitant, I thought back to my days in figure skating. Change required courage, and courage meant pushing through fear and self-doubt. Just as I had faced thousands of falls on the ice, I knew I could face failures on this new path too. And this time, I wasn't alone. My husband and children were my pillars, their unwavering support giving me strength to follow my dreams. The love and encouragement I received reminded me of my parents' belief that growth comes from every experience, success and failure alike.

My first steps into the art world were both exciting and intimidating. I started creating pieces inspired by the sparkly world I'd loved as a figure skater. My art, much like my skating, became a reflection of resilience, determination, and the joy of trying. I knew that taking my work seriously would mean facing rejection, putting myself out there, and braving the fear of failure all over again. The first time I approached a gallery with my art, I felt the same rush of nerves I'd felt before performing on the ice. But I remembered the lesson I always tell my children—that the outcome isn't as important as the effort. What mattered was that I tried my hardest.

To my surprise, my art resonated. My work, filled with bold colors, intricate textures, and layers of sparkle, began finding homes in galleries across the country. I'd gone from decorating gym shoes with hot glue, glitter, and rhinestones as a child to creating three-dimensional egg sculptures covered in thousands of fine crystals—sculptures that people now call, "jewelry for the home." Each piece was a celebration of everything I'd learned through skating, medicine, and life: the resilience to keep trying, the courage to embrace change, and the beauty of creating something that sparkles not just visually, but emotionally as well.

The process of creating my art often takes me back to my childhood memories of sitting with my mom on the family room floor, watching her sew Swarovski crystals by the thousands to my skating costumes. She would spend hours after work embellishing those costumes, and I would sit beside her, gluing sequins and rhinestones onto my shoes. We transformed the ordinary into something extraordinary, adding sparkle to everything, because plain, simply, wasn't good enough. My mom's patience, her attention to every detail, taught me about dedication and the magic that happens when you add a little extra shine to life. My dad always offered steady encouragement. He was the voice reminding me that perseverance and a positive attitude could get me through anything. Looking back, I see how these memories shaped my journey and inspired me to create something meaningful.

Today, as a full-time artist, I feel deeply grateful for the support and love that helped me reach this point. My art is more than a creative expression; it's a tribute to the lessons of resilience and determination I've learned along the way. Every sculpture I create is infused with the spirit of my skating days and the belief that life, like art, is about embracing change, facing challenges, and adding a touch of sparkle wherever possible.

I often share these values with my children, encouraging them to give their best in everything they do and to find courage in the face of fear. I remind them, as my parents reminded me, that success isn't defined by the end result but by the effort and heart we put into the journey. My hope is that they, too, will learn that every setback, every fall, is an opportunity to rise stronger.

My story—spanning from the icy rinks of Chicago to the vibrant art galleries across the United States—is a journey shaped by resilience, creativity, and the courage to dream. Each piece of art I create is a testament to the belief that we can all rise after every fall, that we can all shine in our own way, and that life's most beautiful moments often come from the courage to try, again and again. My journey reminds me that with love, hard work, and a little sparkle, we can transform every challenge into something extraordinary.

From Shattered Glass to Unbreakable Spirit: A Journey of Faith, Freedom, and Healing

Arsemiris Galva

As a divorced mom of two boys turned thriving entrepreneur and author, Arsemiris Galva embodies resilience, faith, and transformation. She understands the challenges of navigating life's transitions and adversities, and knows that with determination, divine guidance, and the right support, transformation is within our reach. In just weeks or months, your life can pivot in extraordinary ways, and Arsemiris is here to guide you.

Her mission is to empower women to rise to their highest potential, deepen their connection with the Holy Spirit, and embrace healing through her proven coaching techniques and therapeutic approaches. Whether you're healing from toxic relationships, striving for secure attachments, or seeking clarity in your purpose, Arsemiris meets you right where you are. She offers customized coaching experiences from intimate one-on-one sessions to dynamic group formats tailored to your unique journey.

With a foundation rooted in education and experience, Arsemiris brings both heart and expertise to her work. She holds a master's of science in public service management from DePaul University, is a certified life and master coach, and was invited to be a member of the prestigious Forbes Coaches Council in 2017. She also completed School of Ministry in 2018, recently earned a mental health coaching certification, and is completing a second master's in clinical mental health counseling.

One of her most transformative offerings is the Warrior Sister's Getaway, an annual retreat on some of the world's most beautiful beaches. These sought-after getaways are a chance for women to unplug, heal, and reconnect with themselves in the breathtaking beauty of God's creation. Through reflective practices, powerful coaching, and intentional moments, participants leave feeling renewed and equipped to embrace their next chapter with purpose. Think of this experience as the intersection of faith and mental health.

When she's not inspiring and guiding women, Arsemiris loves traveling, dancing, and creating special memories with her two amazing boys. You'll often find her soaking up the sun on a beach, finding joy in the everyday, and embracing life's spontaneous moments.

https://www.coacharsemiris.com/links

The glass table crashed against the wooden kitchen floor, shattering the fragile illusion of safety I had clung to for far too long. In that split second, my only thought was to protect my five-year-old son and the baby growing inside me—six months into a pregnancy that now felt like an impossible battle. Instinctively, I became their shield, placing my body between them and the chaos. When I looked into my then-husband's eyes, I didn't see the man I once loved; I saw pure rage—an embodiment of darkness I could hardly comprehend.

Deep down, I knew this wasn't the moment for fear or reaction. It was a moment of survival. That April morning in 2017 will forever be etched into my soul, marking the day my life changed forever. It was the day I decided to fight—not just for my children but for myself, my future, and the woman God called me to become.

On paper, my life was a highlight reel of success. I was the epitome of a high achiever—driven, determined, and unwilling to take "no" for an answer. I thrived professionally, transitioning from working in government to founding my nonprofit, launching a successful coaching practice, being invited to join the Forbes Coaches Council, and even venturing into real estate. I was constantly pursuing academic growth, always setting and slaying my goals. To the outside world, I had it all—career success, a growing family, and seemingly everything I could have ever dreamed of.

But behind closed doors, my life was a storm of chaos. I was battling a marriage that was not just toxic but soul-crushing. By 2013, the cracks in my carefully curated image began to show. One cold Chicago afternoon, I found myself gasping for air as if the walls of my car were closing in. My hair started falling out in clumps, my body ached from tension, and my mind raced incessantly. The physical manifestations of anxiety—the word my doctor used to describe the whirlwind I felt inside—terrified me. I felt powerless to stop it.

I wasn't ready to start medication, but the breathing exercises my doctor suggested became a lifeline. Yet, I wasn't just battling anxiety; I was wrestling with a deeper truth. My marriage, the foundation I had built my life upon, was crumbling. Infidelities, abuse, and manipulation left me feeling like the shell of the strong woman I once believed myself to be. I felt trapped, suffocating under the weight of perfectionism and the pressure to maintain an image of strength for my children and for everyone else who relied on me. I had built my life on the façade of control and success, but inside, I was unraveling.

That same year, 2013, I received news that shifted my perspective. My father called, his voice trembling as he said, "*More, tengo cáncer.*" Time seemed to stand still as I processed his words. That moment birthed a cry from my soul—a deep, guttural release of pain, fear, and desperation. It was a cry that would begin a transformation I couldn't yet understand. The man who had always been my rock, my guide, my greatest supporter was now facing his own battle with cancer. It felt as though the world was collapsing around me, and the weight of everything hit me at once.

Later that evening, still reeling from the news, I found myself at a CVS. In one of the aisles, a book seemed to jump out at me. It was about praying boldly. That small, seemingly random encounter was a divine interruption. God met me there, not in a church or at a conference, but in a drugstore, using a book to whisper, "I see you, and I'm not done with you yet." It felt like a small but significant spark in the dark, a flicker of hope in the midst of my deepest sorrow. I walked out of that store with the book in hand, unsure of the road ahead but knowing that I wasn't alone.

By 2015, I had begun an international women's group, The Warrior Sisters Group, a space where faith, coaching, and mental health intertwine. It became a lifeline not just for others but for me as well. Leading this group gave me purpose and reminded me that God could use even my brokenness to help others heal. In the midst of my personal turmoil, I had found a sense of community and mission, helping others while working through my own struggles. Yet, I soon learned that healing wasn't linear.

That same year, I celebrated professional milestones like receiving the 30 Under 30 Award while simultaneously confronting heartbreak. Discovering yet another infidelity shattered my joy and reignited the wounds I had tried so hard to bury. Each success seemed to be paired with a trial, as though life was testing whether I truly believed in the transformation I was fighting for. It was as if life was determined to keep me humble, to test my resilience. The inner turmoil I had been hiding for so long surfaced in full force, making me confront the reality of what I had been enduring in silence.

By 2017, the year the glass table shattered, I was finally ready to walk away. That decision wasn't just about leaving a toxic marriage; it was about choosing life, freedom, and the calling God had placed on my heart. The years of emotional abuse, manipulation, and betrayal had broken me down to the core, but I knew it was time to rebuild. I had spent so many years surviving, but I wanted to thrive. I was no longer willing to accept less than what I deserved.

Leaving wasn't easy. I was a single mother to two young boys, grappling with the emotional and financial challenges of starting over. But every step I took toward healing felt like reclaiming a piece of myself. That year, I was invited to join the Forbes Coaches Council and began speaking and coaching more women who, like me, were navigating the complexities of rebuilding after devastation. It was in that space that I found my true calling—to help others rise from the ashes of their own struggles and find strength in their faith, like a true Warrior Sister.

During this season, the vision for global women's getaways began to take shape. In 2019, I hosted the first Warrior Sisters Getaway—a sacred space where women could unplug, heal, and grow. These retreats are at an intersection of faith and mental health, offering a holistic approach to healing that integrates mind, body, and spirit. Whether standing on a beach or walking through a rainforest, the women who have attended these getaways find freedom in surrendering their pain and reconnecting with God's creation. Through these retreats, I began to see the power of community and the transformative healing that comes from being surrounded by women who have walked similar paths—women who are ready to take deep dives into their life journeys, heal through curated workshops, and grow.

Through the years, Warrior Sisters has grown into a movement. It's not just about gathering women; it's about breaking generational cycles of trauma and building a community rooted in faith, resilience, and empowerment. The getaways are now held in breathtaking locations worldwide, providing women with the opportunity to step away from the noise of life and into a space where healing can begin. What started as a personal mission has grown into something much larger than I could have ever imagined. The women who attend these retreats are not just healing—they are becoming catalysts for change, for their families, their communities, and future generations.

As I reflect on my journey, one truth stands out: adversities are not meant to destroy us; they are meant to refine us. The trials I've faced—from a broken marriage to health challenges, heartbreak, and the weight of starting over—have shaped me into the woman I am today. They've taught me that healing is not a one-time event but a lifelong journey, and that true strength comes not from avoiding pain but from confronting it with courage and faith. It's in our weakest moments that we often find our greatest strength, and I have learned to embrace every part of my story, even the painful chapters.

I've learned that our greatest battles often precede our greatest breakthroughs. The glass table that shattered on that April morning in 2017 didn't just mark the end of a chapter; it marked the beginning of a new one. It was the day I chose to stop surviving and start thriving. That day, I made the choice to break free from the chains of fear and pain that had held me captive for so long. I chose to reclaim my life, my purpose, and my true identity in Christ. I chose to break the cycle of harmful patterns, beliefs, and behaviors that had been passed down through generations within my family and community. It was time to make a conscious effort to heal and create healthier patterns for my future generations. I took time to nurture my faith and heal in the areas of attachment styles, emotional intelligence, and family dynamics; this allowed me to develop a deep understanding of who I am.

Today, as the founder of Warrior Sisters, I have the privilege of walking alongside women who are choosing the same path. Together, we are rewriting our stories, breaking chains, and building legacies of hope and healing. My life's mission is to remind every woman that no matter how dark the night, there is always a dawn. No matter how shattered you may feel, there is always a way to rebuild. You are never too broken to rise.

So, to every woman reading this: know that you are not alone. You are stronger than you think, braver than you feel, and more capable than you realize. Adversity may challenge you, but it will never define you. You were made to rise. And when you do, you will not just survive—you will shine. Your story is still being written, and it's one of resilience, transformation, and victory. Trust the process, lean into your faith, and know that the best chapters are yet to come for you and your future generations.

The Porcelain Doll

Melissa "Mel" Green

Melissa "Mel" Green's story is one of resilience, empowerment, and purpose. Growing up in East Lansing, Mich., her life appeared picture-perfect: an elite gymnast, a dedicated student, and part of a loving family. Yet, behind her success lay struggles with self-doubt, depression, and disordered eating, battles that nearly broke her but ultimately ignited her drive to help others.

Mel's gymnastics career taught her discipline and perseverance, qualities she carried into her legal journey. After earning her law degree from the University of Michigan, she built a twenty-year legal career, including sixteen years in-house advising senior executives. In 2022, she launched MDG Law Virtual, a firm dedicated to empowering solopreneurs and small businesses to thrive by protecting their ventures and navigating legal challenges.

Her passion for service extends beyond law. In 2020, she founded EverGreen Dreams, a nonprofit providing scholarships and mentorship to young Black women through the Building Opportunities for Sistas to Shine (B.O.S.S.) Scholarship. This initiative embodies her belief in the power of intentional action to create lasting change.

Today, Mel embraces her guiding principles of empowerment, intentionality, and soaring beyond limits. No longer a porcelain doll, she draws strength from her experiences to uplift others. Whether through her law firm, nonprofit, or advocacy, Mel is committed to helping others shine.

When not serving her clients or community, Mel enjoys traveling and creating memories with family and friends, embodying her values of connection, excellence, and empowerment.

Instagram: @mdglawvirtual

Website: www.mdglawvirtual.com

Growing up in a middle-class family in East Lansing, Mich., my life may have appeared to some as picturesque. Surrounded by friends and recognized as a talented gymnast at a young age, I seemed to embody happiness and success. By the age of seven, following in my older sister's footsteps, my mother enrolled me at Great Lakes Gymnastics Club and I quickly ascended to become one of the top gymnasts in Michigan.

From the outside, I was the picture of joy and confidence. But on the inside, I felt like a porcelain doll—polished, poised, confident, and happy on the surface, but on the inside, I was fragile, empty, and often telling myself that the world would be better without me.

No one knew the darkness I carried within me. I concealed my pain behind a carefully maintained facade, afraid of judgment and misunderstanding. This marked the beginning of my habit of smiling through the pain, shutting people out, and suffering in silence.

My journey from being a fragile porcelain doll to being the resilient, purpose-driven woman I am today has been marked by falls and rises from the ashes. Now, as the founder and managing attorney of my own solo law firm and the executive director of a nonprofit that provides scholarships to two young Black women graduating from high school, my life is filled with light, joy, and happiness.

Now that you have the background, let me tell you the whole story. Picture it, East Lansing, Mich. I grew up a stone's throw away from Michigan State University with two college professor parents, and an older sister I idolized. Education, family, and gymnastics formed the foundation of my early years.

As a younger sister, I wanted to emulate everything my sister did. They say imitation is the sincerest form of flattery, but I'm pretty sure my sister was just annoyed! While she may not have been flattered, my desire to follow her led me to gymnastics. Although most elite gymnasts begin training at two or three, I was almost seven by the time I stepped on the floor for my first gymnastics class. Yet, I quickly caught up, dedicating twelve to fifteen hours a week to training by age eight. Gymnastics wasn't just a hobby; it was a way of life. No more *Muppet Babies*, no *She-Ra* or *Smurfs*, and no *Looney Tunes* for me. My days revolved around leotards, chalk, and sweat, and I loved it. But as I moved from fifth grade to sixth grade, the joy gymnastics gave me could not drown out the darkness inside me.

I vividly remember sitting in my sixth grade social studies class writing my first letter describing how I believed that "if I was no longer here—no one would even miss me." I remember the tears I choked back and the feeling of profound emptiness. When the bell rang, I folded the letter into my pocket and went about the rest of that day as though nothing was wrong. No one watching me would have known that I was counting the minutes until I could get home and end the excruciating sadness that engulfed me with a bottle of pills.

At the same time, I was beginning to dream of becoming a lawyer. My mother insists my desire stemmed from my sister wanting to be a doctor, and her declaration that I couldn't be a doctor like her. Allegedly my mother suggested, "Then you can become a lawyer instead." I, however, attribute my decision to watching Blair Underwood on *LA Law* and imagining myself working alongside someone like him! Either way, that early decision planted a seed that would shape my future.

By age 13, I was a member of the U.S. Elite National Team, representing the U.S. in international competitions, and aspiring to compete in the '96 Olympics. Yet, I was also battling bulimia. The physical "high" I felt after purging trapped me in a dangerous cycle, leaving me addicted to the fleeting euphoria.

A severe back injury at 14 shattered my Olympics dreams, so I recalibrated my goals and focused on collegiate gymnastics instead. In addition to physical setbacks, I continued to battle my personal demons. By 16, I was a full-blown bulimic, concealing my struggles from everyone. On my not-so-sweet 16th birthday, I overdosed on diet pills, collapsing at school, and was rushed to the hospital. That moment became a turning point, marking the first time I admitted out loud, "I have a problem, and I need help."

As a freshman on the Michigan State women's gymnastics team, I was determined to keep the secrets I had been hiding since middle school to myself. Once again, I was leading a seemingly picturesque life, but in reality, I remained that porcelain doll who was suffering in silence.

Gymnastics taught me discipline, perseverance, and mental toughness—qualities that prepared me for the rigors of law school. Through all the adversity in my four-year collegiate career, I pushed forward. Gymnastics ingrained in me the resilience to rise after every fall, a lesson I carried into my legal career.

After graduation from MSU, I attended the University of Michigan Law School. After graduating from law school, I started my career in a Cincinnati law firm before transitioning to in-house counsel roles. I enjoyed the intellectual challenge of partnering with senior executives, learning business strategies, and developing contracts that supported strategic goals. However, not all experiences were positive.

The first defining moment of my career came in January 2013. During a one-on-one meeting, my manager told me he couldn't think of a single valuable contribution I had made in the prior year. His words stung deeply, but they also lit a fire within me. That Friday as I walked home to my D.C. apartment, I decided to resign. By Monday, I submitted my resignation, vowing never to remain in an environment where I wasn't valued.

Fast forward to October 2021, another turning point in my legal career arrived. My beloved general counsel announced he would be departing in March 2022. That announcement prompted me to reevaluate my path. I had already started building my law firm as a side business. During a conversation with a colleague, she said, "Why don't you just run the law firm full time? When are you ever going to have this kind of opportunity again?" And it was in that moment that I decided to take the leap, and in July 2022, MDG Law Virtual officially launched.

The inspiration for my nonprofit, EverGreen Dreams, came during the pandemic, following the heartbreak and frustration I felt in the wake of George Floyd's tragic death. Watching police in riot gear march down my street toward Michigan Avenue broke my spirit but also sparked a desire for change. I decided I couldn't remain a passive observer.

I founded EverGreen Dreams to empower young Black women through education and mentorship. Our Building Opportunities for Sistas to Shine (B.O.S.S.) scholarship provides financial support and guidance to help them thrive. Witnessing the first scholarship recipients prepare for graduation reaffirms my belief in the power of intentional action.

Empowerment, intentionality, and soaring beyond limits are more than just words to me—they are my guiding principles. Growing up, I struggled with feelings of inadequacy and depression, often believing the world would be better without me. Those dark times fueled my desire to use my voice and talents to empower others, especially young Black women, to embrace their power and walk boldly in their greatness.

Intentionality allows me to align my actions with my values. Whether coaching gymnastics, mentoring young professionals, or running my businesses, I approach each endeavor with purpose.

Starting a solo law firm hasn't been without its hurdles. Finding clients remains an ongoing challenge, but I've learned to adapt by partnering with freelance legal organizations and leveraging my network. Doubts still creep in, but I persevere by seeking guidance from mentors, leaning on my family, and simply doing the work. Sometimes, you have to fake it until you make it.

As a lawyer, I strive to make my clients feel protected, valued, and supported. As a nonprofit leader, my goal is for EverGreen Dreams to outlive me, continuing to uplift young Black women for generations. My message to aspiring lawyers and young women is simple: Find a path that aligns with your spirit. Go where you're celebrated, not tolerated, and never let anyone dim your light.

Today, I no longer see myself as a porcelain doll. I've embraced my cracks, filled them with gold, and transformed into something far stronger and more beautiful. Like the phoenix, I have risen from the ashes of my challenges, soaring beyond limits I once thought insurmountable. My journey is far from over, but I now walk it with purpose, resilience, and the joy of helping others shine.

A Life's Work: Understanding Food Allergies, Advancing Medicine, and Advocating for Change

Dr. Ruchi S. Gupta

Ruchi Gupta, MD, MPH, is a Professor of Pediatrics and Medicine at Northwestern University Feinberg School of

Medicine and a Clinical Attending at Ann & Robert H. Lurie Children's Hospital of Chicago. Dr. Gupta has 20 years of experience as a board-certified pediatrician and health researcher and currently serves as the founding director of the Center for Food Allergy & Asthma Research (CFAAR). She is world-renowned for her groundbreaking research in the areas of food allergy and asthma epidemiology, most notably for her research on the prevalence of pediatric and adult food allergy in the United States. She has also significantly contributed to academic research in the areas of food allergy prevention, socioeconomic disparities in care, and the daily management of these conditions. To reduce the burden of these diseases and improve health equity, she and her team develop, evaluate, and disseminate interventions for families and conduct work to inform local, national, and international health policy. Along with being an author of The Food Allergy Experience and Food Without Fear, Dr. Gupta has over 200 publications and her work has been featured in major TV networks and print media. To learn more, visit cfaar.northwestern.edu.

www.yobeecare.com
Instagram: @Yobeecareofficial
Twitter: @Yobeecare
TikTok: @Yobeecare
https://www.facebook.com/YobeeCare
https://www.linkedin.com/company/yobeecare/

There are moments in a career and life when a single experience shifts the course of everything. For me, the work I had been doing in my research lab and clinic, now entered my own home. As a new mom, I held my daughter as she struggled with relentless skin and scalp issues. I had spent years training as a pediatrician, studying the atopic march, yet I found myself searching for answers in ways I had never anticipated.

What I discovered—what so many families already lived— was the incredible impact eczema has on all aspects of life, with limited treatments and solutions and with the all too often progression into food allergies. This was an urgent and growing public health issue, and my path to impact became clear.

My early passions were science, curiosity, service, connection, and acting. Medicine seemed like a natural path for the first four at least. As I went through medical school, I was drawn to developing projects and leadership in organizations to make change happen. I loved working with high school students and was drawn to mentoring. This is where the fourth passion of acting came through with public speaking on important health topics. That led me from medical school at the University of Louisville to a residency in pediatrics at the University of Washington, then to a research fellowship at Harvard.

At Harvard, I began to see how research could be a force for change. Medicine isn't just about treating the patient in front of you—it's about looking at patterns, asking questions, and using data to improve lives on a larger scale.

The first question that needed an answer was, What is the public health impact of food allergies in the United States? We knew food allergies were on the rise, but no one had quantified the impact.

In 2011, my team and I conducted the most significant epidemiological studies on food allergies in the United States. What we found changed the national conversation: 1 in 13 children—roughly two in every classroom—had a food allergy. That statistic became a defining moment, not just for me as a researcher, but for families and policymakers across the country.

Our research went deeper, uncovering the economic impact of food allergies, which was estimated at nearly $25 billion per year when factoring in medical costs, emergency room visits, special diets, and lost productivity. We saw how these allergies didn't just affect children but shaped the lives of their families—

determining where they could eat, where they could travel, and how they navigated the world.

Facts and figures alone don't create change—action does. That's why I founded the Center for Food Allergy & Asthma Research (CFAAR) at Northwestern University Feinberg School of Medicine and Lurie Children's Hospital of Chicago. Our mission is to turn what we know into solutions: better policies, better treatments, and better education for families, schools, and communities.

One of our most significant achievements was working with Chicago Public Schools to implement policies ensuring that schools had access to emergency epinephrine. For the first time, schools were prepared to handle life-threatening allergic reactions, even if a child had no prior diagnosis. That policy became a model for other school systems and, eventually, for federal legislation.

Seeing these challenges firsthand, I realized that medical research alone wasn't enough—families needed real, accessible solutions. Science is about discovery, but innovation is about applying those discoveries in ways that make a difference. That belief led me to an unexpected chapter in my career: entrepreneurship.

Yobee Care was born of necessity. I worked with leading dermatologists, allergists, and microbiologists to develop a solution for my daughter's eczema and cradle cap, shared it with our patients for 10 years, and now sharing it with the world. Yobee was born out of love, with the wisdom of nature, and perfected by science. After clinical studies in adults and children, we found that Yobee products (scalp mask, shampoo, conditioner, and face and skin cream support skin and scalp microbiome and decrease irritation and itching in all age groups. Our goal is to support the skin's natural barrier with safe, healthy products for the whole family.

Every day, I meet parents, children, doctors, researchers, and policymakers who share a common goal: to make life better for the millions of people living with eczema, allergies, and asthma. The work isn't finished—there is still so much to understand, from the root causes to potential treatments and even cures. We are moving forward, step by step, armed with knowledge, driven by data, and, above all, guided by the people we serve.

Medicine is more than science. It's more than research. It's about impact. How do we create lasting change in health? My hope is that today's work will build a future where no child fears the food they eat.

That is why I do this work. That is why this is my life's mission.

Becoming… Me

Shatesha Holder

Shatesha Holder launched her interior design business, Staging Spaces Inc. in 2016, and has made a name for herself as one of Chicago's Black Luxury Interior Designers. In 2016, she received certification and training in home staging and redesign. Her firm's focus is curating beautiful, functional spaces. Although based in Chicago, Ill., Shatesha enjoys traveling throughout the United States to bring her clients' visions to reality in their homes and businesses. As Staging Spaces continues to grow, she's had the pleasure of designing several commercial spaces, including a dental office in Texas, a children's hair salon, and even a restaurant. Shatesha is firm in her belief that time management is her superpower. She wears many hats, including being a wife, mom, corporate leader, and interior designer, but her favorite thing to do is spend time with her family.

Instagram: @staging.spaces
https://www.stagingspaces.net/

My journey has been quite an adventure—not always fun, but thrilling and complex. Along the way, I've met more versions of myself than I could have ever imagined.

It was December of 2014. Chicago was briskly cold as usual, and I had the grand idea of leaving my wonderful job of four years at a very prestigious St. Louis University to re-locate back home to Chicago. Being homesick had finally gotten the best of me—but honestly, I was also looking for "more." I wasn't sure what the "more" was at that time; I just knew part of it included more money. My career in clinical research was great. It was steady. It was comfortable... maybe too comfortable. I worked hard, but no longer felt challenged. At that time, there was no real room for growth within my organization. All of my coworkers were older than me, and they had no desire to climb the corporate ladder. Their career ambitions were drastically different from those of my then-twenty-eight-year-old self. I knew that at some point, I wanted to start a family, and my idea of work-life balance did not involve me coming into an office every day. I started hearing so much buzz about how the pharmaceutical industry had tons of remote jobs. Working from home wasn't a big thing at that time, so I thought. I soon landed a new job back home in Chicago, with another large university.

I had a beautiful going away party in St. Louis, both at work and privately with close friends. My life in those four years was full of joy, lots of work (at one time I worked three jobs while getting my second master's degree), and solitude. I had my weekly routines of going for four- to six-mile runs in Forest Park and visiting the farmer's market in Soulard. I built thriving friendships, which are still very strong to this day. St. Louis really helped shape my adult years, but it was off to Chicago! This big city girl missed home and family.

Returning home was full of gut punches. The great job that I accepted was nothing short of a disaster. Talk about a toxic work environment! After nine months, I moved on and joined big pharma. I was greeted with a well-deserved generous pay increase, but it came with a long work commute: two hours each way to be exact, but I got my foot in the door. I settled into that role for a while, but then there was still that thing thumping in the back of my mind, *You can do more. You can do more for yourself. Chase your own dreams. Umm... what exactly is my dream, anyway*, I thought. *Am I only focused on my corporate career? What about things that are fulfilling and bring me joy outside of work?*

Quick backtrack. When I got my first apartment in college, I discovered my love for decorating. I had the cutest apartments! I also fell in love with what is still my absolute favorite store, Hobby Lobby. My love for home décor continued to grow, and I eventually started decorating for family members. It was just simple things like decorating towels in their bathrooms and creating floral arrangements.

Jump back to 2015, I sat and talked with my best friend, who I can always count on for a bit of encouragement. (If you let her in on any idea that you have on elevating your life, she'll push you to your full potential. We all need a friend like that!)

My friend gave me the bright idea of starting a home staging business. *Are you crazy!?* I thought. At first, that idea completely frightened me! I knew nothing about a business, let alone having people actually pay me—but then I thought, *wait a minute, maybe she's onto something!* The more I thought about it, and the more she pushed, her idea didn't seem so far-fetched. In fact, I loved it! Then I wondered, *where do I start*? Because she was in the process of starting her own business, she suggested that I join the next cohort of the business builder's workshop with her at a local chamber of commerce in Chicago. I got to work on my business plan and enrolled in a class to receive my certification in home staging and redesign. I pitched the idea to my family, and it was well received, but I could not decide on a business name. I pondered on it for weeks and finally my friend suggested, "You should call your business Staging Spaces!" She had a ton of catchy slogans and phrases to go along with it. Boom, that was it! I found the "more."

After going through the classes, becoming certified, and working with lawyers to develop my contract, my business became incorporated in April 2016. Meanwhile, I met the love of my life. He came right in and encouraged me even further with my business pursuits. I began putting my business hat to work by starting with my own home. To my surprise, my first actual client was located in New Orleans, not Chicago. I gained more clients here and there, and then bam, I became a mom in 2018! My beautiful baby girl was the missing piece to our puzzle. This was the most beautiful time of my life, and now another version of myself that I had to learn: from corporate girly to business owner, and now mommy. Oh, did I mention that we also bought a house right before our daughter was born? At this point, my life had become so full that I didn't see where my business could fit in. I continued climbing the corporate ladder and landed a higher role just when my daughter was three months old. There I was flying to in-person meetings, stepping away to use my breast pump, and bringing my mother and baby along on the work trips. Where would I have time to decorate anyone's home? I decided not to send my daughter to daycare, and I homeschooled her for three-and-a-half years before we sent her to preschool. As you can probably guess by now, my business was in a full hiatus for nearly three years.

I jumped back into things in 2021, and boy, did it take off quickly. I ended the year with over sixteen completed projects.

In 2022, I had a beautiful destination wedding and here I am again with a new version of me: wife. (Insert big smile here.) Oh yeah, we bought another house! Business continued to grow at a steady pace, and in 2021, I began working on commercial projects, and traveling out of state to work on client spaces.

I'd like to take a short pause here to acknowledge my mom. From my early childhood, I remember our apartments always being beautifully decorated—above average of what you'd expect an apartment to look like. She hired people to install wallpaper in our rooms, and my princess-themed bedroom with a curtain-draped canopy bed looked like something out of a magazine. The love for décor was always in me.

Over the years, my knowledge and skills have drastically changed for the better and I vow to always remain a student and be teachable in this industry. I've had the pleasure of managing large and small contracting teams, working with architects, and bringing on an assistant and intern. My business and client base have grown to something I am truly proud of, but what I take the most pride in is my ability to juggle it all. While my business has now grown into a boutique interior design firm, I still enjoy the stability of being in the corporate world. I very often hear from others, "I don't know how you do it all." To be honest, early mornings are my secret weapon. My mornings are first spent with God, then Staging Spaces, and then corporate. I place a heavy emphasis on having family time and being present. Although this is a very short version of my story, I hope that it may be of encouragement to a reader who is searching for their "more." Please always know that it's already in you. You can have it all, with hard work and dedication. You can balance it all, with the proper mindset and the skill of time management. God Bless.

I'd like to dedicate this chapter to my amazing mother-in-love who transitioned to be with God late last year. Thank you for your unconditional love, support, and believing in me beyond what I could see. You are deeply loved and missed.

Shattering Shame

Heather Huffman

Heather Huffman is the co-owner and managing partner of Lena's Social Club, a restaurant and catering company in Dixon, Ill. With a passion for bringing people together, Heather and her husband, Greg, have created a space where great food and a sense of community come together. Heather's background in customer service, training, marketing, and sales, combined with Greg's experience in restaurant management, has allowed them to cultivate an environment where kindness and care are at the heart of everything they do.

Raised in Dixon and with over 26 years in the Kansas City suburbs, Heather returned to her hometown with Greg to invest in the community they love. She's committed to running Lena's

Social Club with integrity and a deep desire to give back to the people of Dixon. Heather's entrepreneurial journey began in the corporate world, where she gained invaluable experience leading teams and building a culture of care.

In addition to her work at Lena's, Heather has a history of service, including founding a free dance ministry for children and advocating for addiction recovery at the Missouri State Legislature. She's dedicated to helping others share their stories and embrace healing, empowerment, and connection.

When not working, Heather enjoys spending time with her family, spoiling her pets, and reconnecting with her childhood best friends. With aspirations to transition into writing and speaking, Heather is focused on empowering others to live authentically and fearlessly.

www.lenasocialclub.com
Instagram: heatherkhuffman
Facebook: Heather (Finn) Huffman
Instagram/Facebook: Lena's Social Club

My story is one of breaking free from the chains of shame, finding healing in the love of community, and learning to love myself in the process. For so long, I carried the weight of believing I wasn't good enough, that my mistakes defined me, and that I was unworthy of peace and joy. But I have learned that healing is possible, and it's never too late to experience freedom. Shame doesn't have to be the story we live out—it can be shattered, and we can rise stronger, loved, and redeemed. This is my journey of shattering shame.

I was the youngest of five children, and from a young age, I was incredibly dependent on my parents. They provided for me in every way, but I leaned on them so heavily that I didn't learn how to navigate life on my own. When things went wrong, they fixed it. I didn't develop the skills needed to make decisions for myself or take care of myself. They loved me very much, and I never doubted their love, but the lack of independence made me ill-prepared to face the difficulties life would throw my way.

As a teenager, I started to compare myself to others, always feeling like I didn't measure up. I felt a sadness inside me I didn't understand at the time and I began to question my own worth—it seemed like no matter what I did, I wasn't enough. I tried to hide that shame through performance, by always being the one to smile and act "happy" all the time. I was very involved in high school activities—cheerleading, student council, and jazz show choir—always striving to excel, to be the one people liked. But the truth is, I was masking a deep sense of insecurity.

And that led me into starting an unhealthy relationship with food, which I used as my coping mechanism. I spent three years binge eating and gained 40 pounds between my sophomore and senior years. That led me to hate myself. I isolated myself and was depressed. I had developed an eating disorder that was driven by the shame I couldn't name. It wasn't just about the food—it was about my need to feel in control of something, anything, in my life.

I was a competitive dancer as well, and that world only magnified my feelings of inadequacy. I constantly scrutinized my own body, comparing myself to others, and feeling ashamed of what I saw. In a culture where appearance mattered, I believed that my worth was tied to how I looked. The more I compared myself to others, the more I internalized shame. I didn't know how to stop the cycle of self-criticism. It was a vicious cycle— every time I didn't meet the ideal standard in my mind, the shame grew.

The shame wasn't just about my appearance—it started to seep into every area of my life. I believed that I was bad, unworthy, and not enough. If something bad happened to me, it meant I was bad. If I made mistakes or choices I regretted, I believed I was unworthy of love or happiness. Shame ruled my life. It was an invisible force that dictated how I saw myself and how I interacted with the world.

Despite my weight gain, at 17, I started my first serious relationship. The relationship was far from healthy, but we were codependent and stayed together despite many people telling us we should go our separate ways. At that time, I started to abuse laxatives to undo the consequences of my binge eating. At my worst, I was downing 100 laxatives at a time and to this day, doctors aren't sure how I didn't end up killing myself with that dangerous behavior. I felt unhappy, and I didn't want to be alone so I ended up getting married right out of college—I was only 21. We were young and naive, and though we both tried to make it work, we were unhealthy individually, which ultimately led to the breakdown of our marriage. I eventually left my marriage, which led to more shame. This is when I started starving myself. I started to feel like I had control, and I remember feeling "clean" when I was thin and "dirty" when the number on the scale wasn't what I wanted it to be.

I was miserable and alone, and I felt like I let everyone down. I wanted to fix it all, so I went back to my ex-husband. We remarried and eventually had two beautiful kids. But something still wasn't right, and I ended up leaving again, which caused more shame. After two divorces, I was left feeling broken and completely lost. Divorce wasn't something I thought I'd ever experience, and I couldn't escape the constant weight of feeling like I had failed—both myself and everyone around me, especially my children.

Food continued to be my coping mechanism. I felt proud when I could starve myself, but when I ate or the number on the scale didn't meet my unrealistic expectations, I hated myself even more. I had developed an eating disorder that was driven by the shame I couldn't name. It wasn't just about the food—it was about my need to feel in control of something, anything, in my life.

When I got divorced for the second time, I swore I wasn't going to date anyone for at least two years. But life had a way of surprising me. Through a mutual friend on Facebook, I met someone who, ironically, grew up in the same small town I did, yet we had never crossed paths until that moment. I was hesitant at first—how could I possibly be ready for another relationship so soon? But as we got to know each other, I realized he accepted me for who I was, not the version I thought I had to be. He saw me beyond my past and the shame I carried, and that gave me hope.

Still, the judgment and assumptions about dating so soon after a divorce brought more shame. I wasn't prepared for the scrutiny that came with being in a relationship so soon. It felt like every decision I made was under a microscope, and it made me retreat further into myself. I couldn't escape the sense of being judged for my past, for my mistakes. But this time, I was determined not to let shame dictate my life anymore. With his support and the love of my friends and family, I slowly began to believe that I was worthy of a second chance. We were married a year and half after meeting, and our marriage has had its ups and downs, just like any marriage does. Greg noticed my unhealthy eating patterns and had a very hard but loving conversation with me. Through his support, I stopped using laxatives, stopped over-exercising (at one point I was exercising four hours per day and consuming only 800 calories), and over time, I learned to have a much healthier relationship with food and my weight, but it is something I always have to work on.

At the time I went through my divorce, I was also navigating the challenge of being a stay-at-home mom who had to start over. After my second divorce, I moved myself and my kids in with my parents and felt like a failure. I was terrified of what the future would hold. I hadn't been in the workforce for years, and I felt an intense pressure to catch up with women who had built successful careers during that time. I pushed myself harder than I ever had before. Within a decade, I went from working as a customer service representative in a small insurance office to being the director of a large insurance call center. But even though I had achieved professional success, I still struggled with feelings of unworthiness and doubt.

The real turning point came when I lost my father in 2024. His death was a crushing blow, not only because I had lost someone so close to me, but because I had lost my safety net. My dad had always been my problem-solver, my wise counselor, and my hero. Watching him lose his memory to dementia, and seeing him not recognize my mother and me, was a painful reminder that life can be unpredictable and cruel. I wasn't just mourning the loss of a father—I was mourning the loss of a part of myself. He was the one I turned to for advice, the one who knew me better than anyone, because I am so much like him. His absence left a hole that felt impossible to fill.

But through the pain, I found my purpose. I wanted to turn my grief into something meaningful, something that could help others. It was through this period of loss and healing that the idea for Lena's Social Club was born. I wanted to give back to the community that had been so good to me when I was growing up. I also wanted to be close to my best friends, whose lives I hadn't been part of in over 25 years due to my own shame and isolation.

When we moved back to our hometown, I was welcomed with open arms by the very people I had distanced myself from. Their love was healing in ways I never expected. It was like they had been waiting for me to return, and through their support, I learned that healing doesn't just come from within—it comes from community. It was a beautiful reminder that no matter how long we've been away, love has the power to heal brokenness and bridge the gap.

Lena's Social Club is more than just a business to me. It's a legacy, a place where we serve not only food but kindness and community. The restaurant is named after the women who shaped our families—my great-grandmother Lena Anderson, Greg's grandmother Lena Huffman, and my mother Harlena Finn. Their love and strength are the foundation of our business.

We named the restaurant after them to honor their influence and the values they exuded: kindness, service, and family.

At Lena's, we serve upscale comfort food, but we also serve kindness. We've created a space where people feel like they belong, no matter where they come from or what their past holds. I've learned that healing and grace are not about perfection but about accepting and loving ourselves through all of our flaws. This is the story of Lena's Social Club—one of community, love, and grace.

Shame is no longer my story. I am enough, and so are you. No matter where you are in your journey, healing is always possible. We don't have to be perfect to be worthy of love, and we don't have to let shame define us. It's time to shatter shame.

Giving Back

Tiffany Jozwiak

Dr. Tiffany Jozwiak has been helping patients look and feel better for over 25 years. Since 1997 she has been practicing general and cosmetic dentistry; her extensive experience ranging from transforming smiles to correcting bites to reducing dental anxiety.

Along with her dental background, Dr. Jozwiak has been training in facial esthetics for over a decade, constantly updating her skills, investing in the latest state-of-the art technology, and providing patients with unparalleled support and attention. She is a frequent speaker at panels and conferences in the beauty and cosmetic dentistry industry and has been recognized as a female leader in her Chicago community.

Dr. Jozwiak earned her bachelor of science degree from the University of Wisconsin-Eau Claire and her doctor of dental surgery from the University of Minnesota School of Dentistry. She is a member of the ADA, FRVDS, and CDS. Dr. Jozwiak knows that all of her patients have different needs and is committed to catering to the diversity and uniqueness of each one.

www.Ozparkfamilydental.com
@ozparkfamilydental

From a young age, I aspired to be a dentist—a profession that would allow me to make a tangible difference in people's lives by helping them feel better and more confident. Growing up, I was inspired by the strong sense of community around me, from the teachers who guided my education to the coaches who instilled discipline and teamwork, and the local employers who gave me my first opportunities. These relationships shaped my desire to serve the very community that had given so much to me.

The path to fulfilling this dream began with a scholarship to the University of Minnesota School of Dentistry, which I pursued after completing three years of undergraduate studies. It was a significant milestone, one that marked the beginning of my journey into a profession I had long admired. During dental school, I immersed myself in rigorous coursework and clinical training, preparing to take on the challenges of dentistry with confidence and compassion.

After graduation, I had the unique opportunity to work alongside the dentist I had grown up visiting. This experience was incredibly formative, offering me insights into the importance of building relationships with patients and providing high-quality, personalized care. I learned not just the technical aspects of dentistry but also the human side of the profession—

how to listen to patients, ease their anxieties, and create treatment plans tailored to their individual needs.

As I built my career, my personal life also flourished. I moved to Chicago, where I raised my three children. Balancing family life with a demanding career was no easy feat, but it taught me resilience and time management. For a while, I commuted daily to Sycamore to work, but the long drive eventually became unsustainable. I realized that I needed to find a way to continue doing the work I loved while staying closer to home and my children.

This realization led me to purchase a dental practice in Chicago, conveniently located within walking distance of my home and my children's school. This decision was life-changing. It allowed me to integrate my professional and personal lives more seamlessly, providing care to families from the school, church, and neighborhood communities where I was raising my own family. There was something deeply rewarding about treating patients who were also friends, acquaintances, and community members—people with whom I shared a connection beyond the dental chair.

Over the years, I have dedicated myself to helping patients look and feel their best. For more than 25 years, I have practiced general and cosmetic dentistry, specializing in a wide range of treatments, from smile transformations to bite corrections. My work has also included addressing dental anxieties and ensuring that patients feel comfortable and supported throughout their visits. I understand that visiting the dentist can be a source of stress for many, and I've made it a priority to create a welcoming and reassuring environment for everyone who walks through my doors.

In addition to my extensive dental background, I have spent over a decade training in facial aesthetics. This specialized training has allowed me to expand my services and offer patients comprehensive care that goes beyond traditional dentistry. By investing in state-of-the-art technology and continually updating my skills, I have been able to provide cutting-edge treatments that enhance both oral health and overall appearance. Whether it's helping a patient achieve a brighter smile or addressing aesthetic concerns, I approach every case with a commitment to excellence and innovation.

One of the most rewarding aspects of my career has been the opportunity to build long-term relationships with my patients. I've had the privilege of treating multiple generations within the same families, watching children grow up and, later, bring their own kids to see me. These enduring connections are a testament to the trust and rapport I've worked hard to cultivate over the years. I recognize that every patient is unique, with their own concerns, goals, and preferences, and I strive to provide care that is as individualized as the people I treat.

My philosophy of care is rooted in the belief that dentistry is not just about treating teeth—it's about improving lives. A healthy, confident smile can have a profound impact on a person's self-esteem, social interactions, and overall well-being. Understanding this, I take a holistic approach to dentistry, considering not only the immediate needs of my patients but also their long-term health and happiness. Whether restoring a damaged tooth, alleviating chronic pain, or crafting a beautiful smile, my goal is to make a positive difference in every patient's life.

In addition to my work in the clinic, I am deeply committed to staying at the forefront of advancements in dentistry and facial aesthetics. The field is constantly evolving, with new technologies and techniques emerging all the time. To ensure that my patients receive the best possible care, I regularly attend continuing education courses, workshops, and conferences. This commitment to lifelong learning has allowed me to integrate the latest innovations into my practice, from digital imaging and 3D printing to minimally invasive procedures that reduce discomfort and recovery time.

Beyond the technical aspects of my work, I am passionate about creating a positive and inclusive environment for my patients. I understand that dental care can be intimidating for some, and I strive to make every visit as comfortable and stress-free as possible. My team and I take the time to listen to our patients, answer their questions, and address their concerns. We believe that informed patients are empowered patients, and we make it a priority to educate them about their treatment options and oral health.

Over the years, I've had the privilege of witnessing countless transformations. I've seen patients who were once self-conscious about their smiles gain newfound confidence and joy. I've helped individuals overcome years of dental anxiety, enabling them to prioritize their health and well-being. These moments make my work so fulfilling, and they reinforce my commitment to this profession.

As I reflect on my journey, I am grateful for the experiences that have shaped me, both personally and professionally. From my early days in dental school to my current practice, each chapter has been a stepping stone toward fulfilling my mission of serving others. I am especially thankful for the support of my family, colleagues, and patients, who have been an integral part of this journey.

Looking ahead, I am excited about the future of dentistry and the opportunities it holds. Advances in technology, materials, and techniques continue to push the boundaries of what is possible, enabling us to provide even more effective and personalized care. I am committed to staying at the forefront of these developments, ensuring that my patients always receive the highest standard of care.

My journey as a dentist has been one of growth, learning, and service. It is a profession that has allowed me to combine my passion for helping others with my love of science and artistry. Whether I'm transforming a smile, alleviating pain, or simply providing a listening ear, I am reminded daily of the profound impact that dentistry can have on people's lives. As I continue to serve my community, I am inspired by the relationships I've built, the challenges I've overcome, and the difference I've been able to make. It is an honor and a privilege to do this work, and I look forward to many more years of helping patients look and feel their best.

Stepping into Brave

Genesis Hey Krick

Genesis Hey Krick, M.A., CLC, is a dynamic high-performance strategist, executive business coach, and the founder and CEO of Dream Ignite Build. With over a decade of experience, Genesis is passionate about empowering high-achieving women—entrepreneurs, moms, and executives—to unlock their fullest potential, elevate their businesses, and create balance in both their personal and professional lives.

As a high-performance expert, Genesis works with clients who are ready to scale their businesses, break through barriers, and achieve extraordinary success without sacrificing their well-being. Her strategic approach combines mindset, energy management, and sustainable systems to help individuals perform at their best while maintaining a grounded and fulfilling life.

Genesis is also a bestselling author, having written and contributed to five books, including *Unleash Your Potential* and *Slaying Tampa Bay*. A sought-after speaker and media personality, she has been featured on ABC7, Atlanta57, BLOOM TV, and Fox13, sharing her insights on leadership, productivity, and personal growth.

Known for her inspiring approach and hands-on coaching, Genesis is dedicated to guiding women through transformational growth, helping them step into their power and create lasting impact in their careers and lives. When she's not working with clients, Genesis enjoys spending time with her husband and four children, writing, and planning her next adventure over an Americano and cake pops.

www.instagram.com/genesisheykrick
www.linkedin.com/genesisheykrick
www.youtube.com/@dreamignitebuild
www.facebook.com/genesisspeaks
www.genesisspeaks.com

I sat there staring out the window, watching the rain streak down the glass. The sky was heavy, the kind of gray that settles into your bones. It was a typical overcast day in Illinois, and I was deep in thought, running through my next sales pitch to a local hospital. As a regional marketing director, I knew I had to bring my A-game, but my mind was somewhere else.

Then my phone rang, snapping me back to the present. My heart lifted when I saw my mom's name on the screen—I always loved hearing her voice, especially on days like this. She was watching my son, Asher, and I was eager to check in.

"How's it going, sweetie?" she asked.

I sighed, forcing a little enthusiasm into my voice. "I'm okay. Just gearing up for my next meeting."

"Well," she said, her voice bubbling with excitement, "I have something to tell you. Asher took some steps in the walker today!"

I froze. A mix of joy and heartbreak flooded through me. My baby had taken steps—and I had missed it. That moment hit me like a ton of bricks. I was grinding every day, pushing forward, doing everything I could to create a good life for us, but at what cost?

Right then, I knew I had to change my path. I needed to take control of my life, my time, my future. I wanted more than just working to get by—I wanted to build something that allowed me to be present for the moments that mattered most.

That realization sparked something in me. I wasn't going to let my circumstances define me. From that day forward, I made a promise to myself—I was going to create a life on my own terms.

It wasn't easy. I was still working full-time while trying to launch my own business on the side. My days started before the sun came up and ended long after it went down. Planning, strategizing, figuring out every possible way to make this work. There were nights I barely slept, mornings I felt completely drained, but I kept going. I knew this was the only way to build the life I truly wanted.

My parents, supportive as ever, started encouraging me to take a break, to get out and meet someone. But dating? That was the last thing on my mind. I was still healing, still carrying the weight of being a single mom with no support.

But one day, I let my guard down. A family friend suggested I go on a casual lunch date with someone fun. Just once, I told myself. And to my surprise, I had the best time. For the first time in a long time, I was laughing—really laughing. It felt good.

And then, after a few dates, something even bigger happened. He met Asher... and he fell in love with him instantly. Not just in a polite, "Oh, he's cute" kind of way, but in a way that made me see a future I hadn't dared to imagine.

We kept growing together, drawn to each other's ambition, our shared vision for life. Eventually, we got married, and I kept pushing forward with my business while he navigated his own career. There were moments of fear, uncertainty, and financial stress, but we never quit. We held onto our dream—one that revolved around financial freedom and, most importantly, quality time with our family.

Through it all, we grew. Our love grew. Our family grew. We had two more beautiful children, and while life became even more chaotic—sleepless nights, constant responsibilities, barely any time for ourselves—we kept moving forward. There were nights I cried from exhaustion, wondering how I could possibly keep going. But deep down, I knew we were building something that mattered.

Then came the biggest decision yet. One night, we sat down and asked ourselves—what if we left? What if we took a leap and moved somewhere bigger, somewhere with more opportunity? It was terrifying to think about leaving our comfort zone, our families, our support system. But we knew that if we didn't go, we'd always wonder what could have been.

So, we went all in. We bought a *big ass* calendar and started counting down the days. In 2018, we packed up everything we owned, loaded it into a trailer, and moved to Florida.

It was exhilarating. It was terrifying. It was exactly what we were meant to do.

The transition wasn't easy. There were moments of deep homesickness, nights where I longed for the comfort of my parents and siblings. But we found our footing. We plugged into a great church, built new connections, and little by little, created the life we had envisioned.

At first, I tried to be everywhere, do everything, say *yes* to everyone. I wanted to be supermom, a powerhouse businesswoman, the perfect wife. But over time, I learned something important—it wasn't about how much I could do. It was about the quality of what I did. More isn't always better. Less is often more. I redefined success, focusing on what truly mattered.

Then, in 2020, our fourth baby was born, completing our little family. Life kept moving, and so did I. My business continued to grow, my vision expanded, and I found myself stepping fully into my purpose. Looking back, I realize now that every challenge, every setback, every sleepless night led me to exactly where I am today.

And here's what I know for sure—moms are the heartbeat of the home. We set the tone. We shape the future. And we have the power to create the life we want, not just for ourselves but for our families.

Today, my family is thriving. Not because everything was easy, but because I chose to be intentional with my time, my energy, my vision. I'm endlessly grateful for my husband, who stuck with me through every wild, ambitious idea. For my kids, who are my greatest motivation.

There have been countless moments where life forced me to pivot, but every single time, I leaned in instead of backing down. That's the key. We can either let life happen to us, or we can take charge and build something incredible.

Now, as I continue to grow my business, raise my kids, and chase dreams bigger than I ever imagined, I hold onto one truth—**everything always works out the way it's meant to.**

And the journey doesn't stop here. This is just another chapter, another step forward. There will be new challenges, new growth, and new dreams to chase. But if I've learned anything, it's that we are always capable of more than we think. The road ahead is filled with possibility, and I am ready to embrace it all— one intentional step at a time.

A Legacy of Excellence in Luxury Real Estate

Carrie McCormick

Carrie McCormick | Luxury Real Estate Broker
@properties | Christie's International Real Estate

Carrie McCormick is a leading force in Chicago's luxury real estate market, bringing over 25 years of experience and more than $2.2 billion in career sales. As the top individual agent at @properties | Christie's International Real Estate, she has built an unparalleled reputation for delivering results with a white-glove, client-first approach that consistently exceeds expectations.

Recognized among the Top 100 Most Influential Real Estate Agents, Carrie has mastered the art of buying and selling luxury homes through storytelling, believing that every home has a unique story—and it is her job to bring it to life. This approach resonates deeply with buyers, creating an emotional connection that drives success.

Carrie's ability to market and sell luxury properties extends beyond traditional methods. As a top real estate social media influencer, she leverages digital platforms to showcase homes to a global audience, ensuring they receive maximum visibility. Her expertise has been featured in several publications further solidifying her position as an industry leader.

What truly sets Carrie apart is her unwavering commitment to twenty-four/seven availability for her clients. In the fast-paced world of luxury real estate, she understands that opportunities arise at any moment—and she is always ready to provide seamless, high-touch service tailored to the unique needs of high-net-worth individuals.

Beyond her success in real estate, Carrie is passionate about mentoring the next generation of professionals entering the industry. She actively guides and supports young real estate professionals, sharing invaluable knowledge, strategies, and insights to help them build successful careers. Her leadership extends beyond business—she is deeply committed to giving back to the community, supporting various philanthropic causes, and using her platform to make a positive impact.

www.carriemccormickRE.com
https://www.linkedin.com/in/carriemccormick/
Instagram: @carriemccormickrealestate
Facebook: CarrieMcCormickREalEstate

Some people believe they can size someone up in an instant, thinking they understand everything about them at first glance. Those who truly know me recognize that I am a force and there's far more beneath the surface. And for those who don't know me yet—this is my story.

The Power of Perspective

I am a force in the Chicago luxury real estate market, known for my expertise, dedication, and strategic marketing acumen. But what many don't know is that my journey to becoming a top broker wasn't conventional—it was forged through resilience, independence, and an unwavering hunger for success.

A Foundation of Independence and Drive

I grew up in Lake Forest, Ill., where I was known as a "tomboy" with a rebellious spirit. Raised by a single mother who had me at just eighteen years old, I watched firsthand the sacrifices, determination, and resilience required to create opportunities. My mother worked two jobs to provide for our family, instilling in Carrie a relentless drive to work hard and make things happen.

From an early age, I learned the importance of trusting my intuition, making decisions quickly, and relying on myself. This independence shaped the way I approached life and business, making me unafraid of challenges and eager to embrace change. I was always looking ahead, always striving for more, and always pushing myself to be better.

A Career Born from an Unexpected Moment

While one might assume that I always dreamed of selling real estate, that wasn't the case. Instead, I began my career in advertising in the late 1990s. I quickly climbed the ranks, achieving great success and recognition in the industry. Yet, despite reaching the top of my game, I found myself unfulfilled. I wasn't passionate about the work, and I knew deep down there was something more for me.

One fateful day, everything changed. After a particularly tough moment at work, I took a walk through Chicago's West

Loop—a neighborhood that was, at the time, on the cusp of transformation. I stumbled upon a construction site and, driven by curiosity, began peppering the developer with questions. That developer, Tom, explained that he was building a new residential development, with condos starting at $300,000.

My first reaction? I thought he was crazy—no one would buy in that neighborhood. But Tom was impressed by my confidence and insight. He invited me to his office to discuss how I could market the project. By the end of that meeting, I was hired to lead the sales team. That moment marked the beginning of what would become a storied career in luxury real estate.

Mastering the Art of Real Estate

My background in advertising proved to be an invaluable asset in my new field. I knew how to craft a compelling message, create an emotional connection with buyers, and position properties in a way that made them irresistible. The development sold out in record time, and my reputation quickly spread. Soon, I was recruited to work with one of Chicago's largest development teams. From there, I continued to hone my skills, building a personal brand that was synonymous with results, excellence, and unparalleled service.

Lessons That Defined a Career

Over the years, I have learned invaluable lessons that have guided my success. These lessons aren't just about real estate—they are about business, leadership, and what it truly takes to excel in a competitive industry.

Lesson #1: Becoming a Brand Ambassador

Early in my career, I observed what other successful agents were doing and tried to mimic their strategies—balloons on open house signs, baking cookies, handing out branded pens. But something wasn't clicking. It wasn't authentic to me, and more importantly, it wasn't what my clients truly wanted.

That's when I realized that success wasn't about following a formula—it was about crafting a brand that was uniquely mine. I became my own brand ambassador, building marketing strategies that were personal, powerful, and effective. I learned that as an entrepreneur, how you market yourself directly impacts whether a prospect chooses to work with you. My job wasn't about pushing sales; it was about creating the best possible experience for my clients.

Lesson #2: The Power of Patience

Ambition alone isn't enough—patience is key. I knew I wanted to be successful, but I also understood that great things take time. I never stopped trying new approaches, refining my strategies, and learning from my failures. I accepted setbacks as part of the process, always pushing forward, never allowing impatience to cloud my judgment.

I have seen firsthand that when people rush success, they make poor decisions and find themselves unfulfilled. My approach has always been about playing the long game—staying focused, staying steady, and knowing that real results come with time and perseverance.

Lesson #3: Checking the Ego at the Door

Real estate isn't about the broker—it's about the client. I learned early on that success in this business isn't about self-promotion; it's about problem-solving. Clients don't care if an agent is ranked number one or has won countless awards—they want someone who will get the job done.

One experience solidified this lesson for me. I was the fourth broker to interview with a seller, who immediately dismissed me by saying, "I'm sure you're going to tell me that you're the number one broker, just like everyone else who has sat in this chair."

But I did something different. Instead of making it about me, I responded, "Actually, I'm not number one—I'm number three." I then focused on what I could do for him, how I could provide value, and how I could deliver the best service. That honesty and client-focused approach won me the listing.

"The one with the ego did not win—the one that serviced the client did."

The Future of Real Estate, Led by Carrie McCormick

Today, I stand as one of the most respected and sought-after luxury real estate brokers in Chicago. My commitment to excellence, my deep market knowledge, and my ability to create innovative marketing strategies have made me a trusted name among high-net-worth clients, developers, and investors.

I'm not just selling properties—I'm transforming aspirations into extraordinary realities. With a reputation built on integrity, expertise, and an unwavering dedication to my clients, I continue to set new benchmarks in luxury real estate.

My story isn't just about success—it's about resilience, evolution, and the relentless pursuit of excellence. And for those who think they know me, there's always more to discover.

A Passion for Design

Christine Mitchell Roman

Christine Mitchell Roman is the founder and principal of CMD Planning and Design, a full-service luxury and lifestyle design firm that specializes in partnering with clients to create unique and innovative interior design spaces that feel captivating and effortless.

Over the course of her illustrious career spanning more than two decades, Christine has been helping clients achieve their design dreams. What sets her apart is her meticulous attention to detail and her ability to listen to a client's vision while providing fresh perspectives and contemporary design trends.

She is a highly accomplished designer renowned for her expertise in luxury interiors and construction design. Christine has been involved in a diverse array of projects—big and small— and has made a significant impact in prominent design hubs across the United States, including Chicago, Naples, Detroit, and

Aspen. Christine's distinctive aesthetic and passion for detail inspire the imaginations of clients and design enthusiasts alike. By combining design elements from vintage to contemporary, Christine seamlessly creates the unexpected while maintaining a sense of timelessness.

Growing up in a Greek-American family instilled a deep and rich appreciation for culture, art, fashion and design. Her parents' love for antiques and collectible furnishings gave her exposure to esteemed auction houses which continually enlightened her to the grandeur of both American and European art and design. Those roots have formed the designer she is today.

@cmdplanninganddesign
www.cmdplanningdesign.com

My career and interest in art and design began early on. I grew up in a Greek-American household, where my parents instilled a deep and rich appreciation for culture, art, fashion and design. They had a love for antiques and collectible furnishings and made a hobby of collecting art and furnishings from around the world. My parents were instrumental in instilling an appreciation for art and architecture and passionately valuing beauty in their surroundings and home. They exposed me to esteemed auction houses that continually enlightened me to the grandeur of both American and European art and design. Art and culture are deeply rooted in my identity and worldview. I take pride in my rich heritage and apply my passion to each project.

My parents owned and operated one of the largest grossing restaurants in Southeast Michigan. They built an empire based on warmth, quality and excellent customer service. Their business practice emphasized the importance of making their customers happy because happy customers make a business succeed. I carried on this practice from the start of my career and believe that what I learned as a child was instrumental in my achievements. Those roots have formed my success.

After high school, I moved to Chicago to pursue my education. Following college, I began my career as a commercial and contract interior designer and later pursued graduate studies in interior architecture. While learning the ins and outs of the practice, I quickly realized that the key to success is to offer customer service that stands out. As a young designer, I worked with large corporate clients such as Motorola, Chicago Tribune, and Children's Memorial Hospital; this set the foundation of my career in both training and growth. I soon learned that the industry was very competitive and that I needed to offer a more personalized approach that dug deep into the corporate philosophy of the client. The design aesthetic would reflect each company's mission. I began incorporating a more individualized approach and established a goal to treat each client as if they were my only one.

During this time, I eventually settled my roots and married my husband of 28 years. After being blessed with three fantastic children, I decided to put my career on pause to raise and nurture my family. Although becoming a mother was my greatest achievement, my love and passion for design continually played a role in my day-to-day life, and was the basis for starting my company, CMD Planning and Design. I implemented my skills and expertise and dove deep into the commercial design world I had once been a huge part of.

In 2020, as the world shifted, so did the need for commercial design. Businesses were closed with no opening date in sight, and the pandemic forced people to work from home. In addition, spending more time at home forced homeowners to create both a comfortable and luxurious home environment. As the word spread about my own specialty in that area, my business flourished, and I started specializing in residential interiors and renovations. CMD Planning and Design was rebranded as a residential interiors and renovation firm.

While applying aspects of my culture and childhood, I built a business that specializes in crafting fresh, bright interiors with a transitional style that reflects each client's unique personality. Today, my firm offers a comprehensive range of services, including interior design, construction planning, project coordination, and kitchen and bath design. My team prioritizes an organic design process that customizes solutions based on lifestyle needs. I focus on wellness-centric design, incorporating mindfulness spaces. My firm prioritizes developing clear communication with my clients, ensuring that both aesthetic and functional needs are met within the established budget. Our goal is to personalize the design process as transparent and enjoyable as possible for everyone involved.

Our expertise and dedication have not gone unnoticed. CMD Planning and Design has been published in esteemed publications such as *Crains Chicago Business*. In addition, the firm has received several accolades. These honors reflect the firm's commitment to excellence and client satisfaction. This uptick reflects my reputation for delivering exceptional design solutions that resonate with clients.

For continued growth, I believe that it's crucial to adapt to evolving trends, technology, and client expectations. I've always embraced technology and see the importance of educating myself and offering clients state-of-the-art services such as 3D visualization and rendering models. Our firm is also putting a bigger focus on showcasing our work and design philosophy through social media engagement and digital marketing.

As the firm evolves, so does my personal passion for design. My hope is that I leave a mark within the community and teach young designers the significance of basing their practice on a client-centric approach and showing a dedication to creating timeless, personalized interiors.

Frozen to Fearless

Lauren Moreno

After being trapped in a bad marriage and navigating through serious health crises for herself and her daughter, Lauren went back to school to study exercise science and became a nationally certified personal trainer with multiple certifications. She then embarked on a new life as a working single mom. This began Lauren's journey from being frozen in her life to embracing a new, fearless style of living.

Lauren focused on the challenge of raising her kids with a mostly absent father and feeding her soul by growing her business and helping others. She became both physically and mentally strong and loved leading her clients to find their own strength. She traveled alone for both volunteering and personal growth. Lauren's fearless spirit helped her experience the joy of new and exciting adventures while helping others discover their own fearless spirits.

Lauren has been featured in numerous publications and recently shared her fitness and fearless lifestyle expertise on WGN Chicago Today. In 2024, Lauren would face her greatest challenge and would come to know what true fearlessness looks like. She shares her story with the hope of inspiring others to understand how to achieve mental and physical strength to pursue their best lives. Her passion is helping others move their lives from frozen to fearless!

Instagram: @fearlesslivingwithlauren

http://www.fearlesslivingwithlauren.com/

At 24, I stood at the double doors of the synagogue as they opened, not with both of my parents as Jewish tradition would dictate. My father had passed two years earlier after a brutal but valiant battle with heart disease. My dad was a remarkable man who lived fearlessly without complaint, no matter what befell him. I loved him with all my heart, and losing him left a hole in my soul that would take decades to heal.

My relationship with my mother was tenuous at best: she was a withholding presence in my life. My father saw me for who I was; my mother only saw me for what I was not. I walked alone and took a deep breath, which scrunched my shoulders up as the door opened. The photographer caught this moment, and later everyone would comment how I looked so innocent and fearful of being a bride. In actuality, the thought that ran through my head the moment those doors opened and I saw my groom standing at the end of the aisle was, "He's not that nice." That moment would mark the beginning of my frozen life, not knowing who I really was, and not being able to tap into the personal power I had over the trajectory of my life. My fearless moments would come after being in a relationship for 21 years with an unkind, withholding man who had no ability to feel true empathy or love for anyone other than himself.

Six months into my marriage, I was diagnosed with a congenital defect that required immediate surgery. The best doctor qualified to handle my complex case was in Boston. My husband at the time had been fired from his second job, so he came with me begrudgingly. I underwent a seven-hour surgery and two weeks in intensive care, where I lost 20lbs due to being fed through a feeding tube.

When we returned home, I weighed less than 95 pounds and had staples across my abdomen. My ex chastised me for walking hunched over "like an old woman" because he had always admired my good posture. I thought, if I were to leave the marriage, who would want me now that I was "damaged goods"? I was truly frozen, and it would take years before I could begin to thaw.

I stayed in this marriage that seemed outwardly perfect for 21 years. I had my precious son, Max. He was such an incredible gift! My ex and I built an extremely successful law practice together, and the money started to roll in. We built our dream home and went on lavish vacations.

Four years after Max came my daughter Chloe. I fully immersed myself in being a mom to my two beautiful children. We seemed to be the perfect little family. Behind the façade, I was crumbling under the weight of my marriage. We tried counseling several times, but nothing ever changed. My life appeared idyllic, but it would not remain that way.

When Chloe turned five, she was diagnosed with Wilms tumor, a rare form of kidney cancer. Her right kidney would have to be removed. I watched them wheel my smiling baby girl with her Shirley Temple curls into the operating room. I am more spiritual than religious, but I fell to my knees and bargained with God, the Universe, any presence that would listen, to please spare my precious daughter. The surgery went well, and we were told she would need six months of chemotherapy. She was in the hospital for two weeks. I slept next to her bed and refused to leave her side. How could I leave her? I was afraid if I looked away for a moment, she could be gone.

We crafted little stained glass butterflies, played and colored each morning from the time she opened her eyes until she closed them at night. When it was time for her first very potent chemo treatment, the nurse came into the room with a Hazmat suit on and offered us one as well. We refused. I needed Chloe to feel safe and did not want to scare her. As the nurse started to administer the chemo, my ex left the room for a phone call. I knew I was on my own with all that was to come. We traveled to the hospital weekly for six months until she completed her treatment and was finally declared cancer-free! She was tiny and frail, but her spirit was strong. I thought I had dodged every parent's biggest fear; unfortunately, I was very wrong.

After her treatment concluded, Chloe was granted a wish by the Make-A-Wish Foundation. Talking about what she would wish for during the long hours of her chemo treatments had helped us remain positive. Chloe wished to have tea with the princesses at Disney World. The trip was magical! My daughter came to life before my eyes, and my heart was so grateful. I began speaking for the Foundation and did so for 23 beautiful years, sharing my experience and raising funds and awareness for other wish children. This helped me heal and make sense of an unfathomable time in our lives. I was honored to receive The Lifetime Ambassador Award from Make-A-Wish for my work, which reminds me that there is light even in the darkness.

A few years after Chloe's recovery, I turned 40 and was diagnosed with an autoimmune condition. While my condition could be controlled with medication, lifestyle changes could also make a profound impact on my health. Discovering the benefits of regular exercise and proper nutrition started my journey into the world of health, fitness, and wellness! I began working out regularly, became a runner, grew muscles I never knew I had, and grew stronger both internally and externally. I returned to school to study exercise science, and when I finished, I took two national certification exams to become a personal trainer. I learned so much about myself during this time, discovering that I was capable of more than I ever imagined. I became an adventurer and did intense fitness challenges that I mastered with ease, went skydiving (the BEST!), went ice climbing, and realized for the first time in my life that I was strong, capable and...SPORTY! I knew I had to share this gift I had discovered within myself with others and began my career in fitness.

During this time, hurricane Katrina hit New Orleans. Seeing the total devastation there, I knew I had to do something to help. I signed up with Habitat for Humanity and flew to New Orleans by myself to build a house in the 9th Ward. I had zero building skill, but I figured my enthusiasm would make up for my lack of skill. We were a bunch of people from all walks of life, building a foundation and framing a house, trying to make a difference. It was the hardest and most gratifying work I've ever done. I continued to build locally when I returned home, and I sponsored a build with a group of my strongest clients. We put a roof on a house in just one day! Chloe even came to build with me on Mother's Day when she was 16. I was no longer frozen, and well on my way to embracing my fearless spirit!

When I returned from New Orleans, I knew I would need to summon the strength to extricate myself from my marriage. It had been so long since I felt true, kind, and complete love (other than from my children), and I wanted the opportunity to attract that into my life. I had a profession, and I knew we had enough money for all of us to be OK after we split it. I assumed he would still take care of his kids whether we were married or not. I was woefully mistaken.

We agreed to part amicably. He suggested that he move upstairs for the sake of continuity for the children. I agreed. Five days later, a moving truck showed up. He had met a foreign woman and secured an apartment for himself. He filed for the divorce, emptied our bank accounts, cancelled all my credit cards and emptied all the cash we had in a safe in our house. He did not make visitation more than a couple of times over the course of the next year, and instead travelled the world with his new girlfriend.

Our year-long divorce was epic and brutal. He had an advantage, being a lawyer himself and knowing how to work the system. I sold valuable possessions at fire sale prices to be able to live with my kids. Ultimately, I was left with tens of thousands of dollars in legal bills, alimony, and enough to put a down payment on a townhome for myself and my kids. Max went to college in Chicago, and Chloe moved into the townhouse with me. I started building my business and embracing my fearless spirit. I embraced the power of meditation, intention setting and manifestation. Helping others discover their own strength and power fortified my own.

I continued to work, volunteer and discover more about myself. I embraced traveling alone, and came to know myself as good company. A few years later, I sold my townhome and bought a condo in Chicago. Chloe decided to move in with me and start her life in Chicago, too. I left my growing business, but I knew that I needed a big change to fully become fearless. I gathered new clients, trained some old clients virtually and was offered a position as a fitness instructor and personal trainer for a downtown luxury hotel. I was thrilled to make my television debut being featured as a fitness expert on *Chicago Today*. I was back in business! My frozen self began to thaw.

My ex would take me to court many times over 12 years, modifying our agreement each time. I didn't have the funds to keep hiring lawyers to defend myself. I realized I had to choose between fighting or relenting and protecting my peace. It resulted in me losing my home, my car, and my lifestyle. Fearlessly protecting my peace was priceless.

My work was gratifying and my children were thriving. Max had his dream job with Red Bull, became a Freemason, and voluntarily enlisted in the Oregon National Guard. Chloe had a successful career in tech sales and became part of the associate board of Make-A-Wish.

Then, in January of 2023, Max had an MRI because of a problem with his right hand. The diagnosis was unimaginable. He had advanced stage four brain cancer. Max was quickly becoming paralyzed on his right side. He started to walk with a pronounced limp. I took him to San Francisco for brain surgery and sat in the waiting room alone (his dad was off skiing). After surgery, the doctor told me that the tumor was like nothing he had ever seen. They could not remove any of it without killing my precious Max. He told me Max needed to get his affairs in order immediately. As the doctor left, I sobbed alone.

My sweet Max was dying, but he was calm when he received the news. We cried together, but even in grief he said, "Mom, I had a list of things I wanted to accomplish in my life, and I've done them all. It's OK, Mom. I'm ready to do whatever I can in the time I have left." My son was so much more fearless than I was. I was determined to try everything I could to help him.

I found the best brain tumor specialist in the country in Chicago and moved Max into my one-bedroom apartment. When the doctor met Max, I knew he would do whatever he could to save him. Max had radiation five days a week and chemo seven days a week. We sat together at every appointment, and he never complained. We had long, impossible talks about his final wishes, and I tried to remain calm. I assured him that his final arrangements would be as he wanted.

Max's doctor tried every available treatment, and through it all, Max remained positive and full of light. We traveled together, and he even went back to his favorite place on earth, Japan. We celebrated Thanksgiving that year and had so much to be grateful for. The holidays were beautiful with friends and "framily" (chosen family), and we all marveled at the miracle of Max!

In the spring of 2024 it became clear that Max's condition was progressing. Seeing my son struggle was so unbearably painful, yet how could I complain when he was living it and adjusting no matter what was thrown his way? Max turned 34 on May 12, and he passed as I held his hand on June 9th.

I gave the eulogy at Max's funeral and tried to capture the magic that was my son. All the challenges in my life paled in comparison to losing this part of me. He was good, he was truth, he was kindness, he was fun, he was interesting, and he was the bravest human I will ever encounter.

Now that I've shared my story, I hope to have shared several things about me and perhaps even in a broader sense, about life. Fearlessness is not living in the absence of fear. It is knowing you are scared but living your life large anyway. No matter what happens in life, we are faced with two choices: We can freeze or we can be fearless. I believe choosing fearlessness leads to choosing light and ultimately joy. I choose to live my life "broken open," holding my grief along with my gratitude. I am attracting joy and love into my broken open heart. I know that Max resides there and his fearlessness will be with me forever.

Planting the Seeds of Well-Rooted

Jessica Pawlicki

Jessica Pawlicki, NP, is a dedicated healthcare professional and the visionary founder of Well-Rooted, a holistic medical practice specializing in pediatrics, functional medicine, and women's health. With a deep passion for uncovering the root causes of health concerns, she empowers patients and families through a personalized, evidence-based approach that blends functional and conventional medicine.

Jessica's commitment to whole-body wellness goes beyond treating symptoms—she seeks to educate, guide, and support individuals on their journey to optimal health. Through Well-Rooted, she has cultivated a patient-centered practice that prioritizes understanding, prevention, and long-term healing. By integrating the latest medical research with natural and holistic therapies, she ensures that each patient receives comprehensive, compassionate care tailored to their unique needs.

As a leader in holistic healthcare, Jessica is redefining the way medicine is practiced by equipping individuals with the knowledge and tools to take control of their well-being. Her mission is to inspire others to make informed, empowered choices that lead to healthier, more vibrant lives.

www.mywellrooted.com
@wellrootedpediatrics
@wellrootedfm
@wellrooted.women
@thewellrootedaprn

From as far back as I can remember, I knew I wanted to be a nurse. Helping people wasn't just something I enjoyed—it felt like a calling. Growing up in a small community, I was the go-to person among my friends and family whenever someone needed medical advice or needed a listening ear. I was drawn to the idea of being a source of comfort and care, someone who could bring a sense of calm amidst the storms of life. By the time I turned sixteen, my path seemed crystal clear: I began working in a hospital setting as a certified nursing assistant (CNA). That experience solidified my passion. Those early days taught me about compassion, resilience, and the profound connection that can exist between a caregiver and their patients.

Working as a CNA was an eye-opening introduction to the raw, unfiltered world of healthcare. I was immersed in the highs and lows of the human experience, witnessing patients' strength in the face of adversity and the quiet determination of families supporting their loved ones. I also saw the tireless dedication of nurses, who so often held everything together behind the scenes. It was in those moments that I learned the power of presence—

how simply being there for someone could make all the difference. That early exposure fueled my drive to advance my education and make an even greater impact.

I went on to nursing school, where I chose to specialize in oncology and hospice care. This chapter of my career was both deeply rewarding and emotionally challenging. Walking alongside patients and families during some of the most vulnerable moments of their lives taught me invaluable lessons about the human spirit. I learned that healthcare is about so much more than treating symptoms or managing diseases; it's about seeing the whole person—their fears, hopes, and dreams— and addressing their needs with empathy and understanding. This belief became a cornerstone of my approach to healthcare, shaping every decision I made moving forward.

A Personal Turning Point

My professional journey was fulfilling, but it was my personal struggles that truly reshaped my perspective on health and healing. After enduring three miscarriages, I found myself lost in a sea of unanswered questions. The heartbreak was profound, and the lack of clarity from traditional medicine left me feeling helpless. Tests revealed no concrete answers, and the solutions I was offered felt like Band-Aids rather than true resolutions. It was in this void of understanding that I made a pivotal decision: I would take my health into my own hands.

This decision marked the beginning of a transformative journey. I immersed myself in the world of alternative therapies, exploring practices like herbal medicine and Mayan abdominal massage. These approaches felt like a breath of fresh air. They honored the interconnectedness of the mind, body, and spirit in a way that traditional medicine often overlooked. Slowly but surely, I began to heal. Through persistence and a holistic approach, I was able to overcome those struggles and went on to have two healthy, beautiful children.

Becoming a mother was a revelation. The moment I held my firstborn in my arms, I felt an overwhelming sense of joy and purpose. But I also became acutely aware of the gaps in pediatric healthcare. At every turn, I encountered fear-driven decision-making and a lack of informed consent. From vaccinations to managing common illnesses, I saw how often parents were pressured into decisions without being fully educated on their options. It was a wake-up call that I couldn't ignore. I realized that the system wasn't designed to empower families—it was designed to maintain the status quo. Medication was often the default answer, and fear-based messaging left parents feeling confused and powerless.

The Birth of Well-Rooted

In 2018, I took a leap of faith and founded Well-Rooted. The name itself reflects the philosophy that underpins the practice: true health requires strong roots. By addressing the root causes of symptoms, we can nurture the body to thrive, rather than just survive. The creation of Well-Rooted felt like the culmination of everything I had learned, both professionally and personally. It was my way of giving back, of creating a space where patients could find the answers, support, and empowerment they deserved.

Well-Rooted has grown into three branches: pediatrics, functional medicine, and women's health. Each branch represents a crucial part of the healthcare landscape, but together, they form a holistic approach to wellness.

- **Pediatrics**: This branch was born from my desire to redefine what it means to care for children. It focuses on informed consent, education, and natural remedies that prioritize the long-term health of the child. It's about creating a partnership with parents, giving them the knowledge and confidence to make decisions that align with their values.

- **Functional Medicine**: Root cause medicine became a passion of mine during my personal health journey. This branch is dedicated to uncovering the underlying imbalances that contribute to chronic conditions. Whether it's through nutritional counseling, gut health optimization, or lifestyle changes, the goal is always to heal from within.
- **Women's Health**: As someone who has walked the road of loss, healing, and empowerment, I felt it was essential to create a space where women could find compassionate, comprehensive care. From fertility and hormonal imbalances to postpartum wellness, this branch addresses the unique needs of women at every stage of life.

Empowerment through Education

At the heart of Well-Rooted is the belief that knowledge is power. Too often, patients are left in the dark about their own health, relying solely on healthcare providers to make decisions for them. My mission was to change that dynamic.

Every appointment at Well-Rooted is an opportunity for education. I take the time to explain the "why" behind every symptom, test, or treatment option. Together, we uncover patterns, triggers, and solutions that align with the patient's goals and lifestyle. This collaborative approach not only improves outcomes but also builds trust and confidence.

For example, in our pediatric branch, parents are encouraged to ask questions and challenge the status quo. Instead of fearing a fever, they learn about its role in the body's natural healing process. Instead of defaulting to antibiotics, they explore alternatives that support the immune system. Conditions like eczema, constipation, ADHD, anxiety, depression, and tic disorders are often viewed as isolated issues, but at Well-Rooted, we see them as interconnected—all stemming from root causes waiting to be unraveled.

Similarly, in the functional medicine branch, patients learn to view symptoms as signals rather than problems to be silenced. A patient struggling with chronic fatigue might uncover that their symptoms stem from nutritional deficiencies, stress, or an undiagnosed thyroid issue. By addressing these root causes, they can achieve sustainable, long-term health.

Building a Community

Well-Rooted isn't just a practice—it's a community. Over the years, it has become a haven for families and individuals seeking a different kind of care. Our patients come to us not just for answers but for validation, understanding, and empowerment.

This sense of community extends beyond the walls of our office. Through workshops, online resources, and social media, I've been able to reach even more people with the message that they have the power to take control of their health. The ripple effects have been profound, creating a network of like-minded individuals who are challenging the conventional approach to medicine and paving the way for a more compassionate, effective healthcare system.

The Journey to Wellness

The path to unraveling root causes isn't always straightforward. It requires patience, persistence, and a willingness to explore uncharted territory. But the rewards are immense.

At Well-Rooted, we are honored to walk alongside our patients on this journey. Whether it's a child with eczema or an adult grappling with anxiety, we approach each case with curiosity and compassion, knowing that the body holds the answers we seek. By peeling back the layers, we uncover not just the root causes of illness but the potential for vibrant, thriving health.

Every symptom has a story. And at Well-Rooted, we are here to help you write a new one—one where you are empowered, informed, and in control of your health.

Looking Ahead

The journey of Well-Rooted is far from over. Each day brings new challenges and opportunities to grow. My hope is that the practice continues to inspire others to question, learn, and take ownership of their health.

As I reflect on the path that brought me here, I'm filled with gratitude. Every struggle, every lesson, and every triumph has shaped me into the nurse practitioner I am today. From the young girl who dreamed of helping others to the founder of Well-Rooted, my mission has always been the same: to empower, educate, and heal.

The seeds of Well-Rooted were planted in my heart long ago, and now, they've grown into something far greater than I ever imagined. Together, with my patients and community, I'm nurturing a future where health is not just the absence of disease but the presence of vitality, balance, and hope.

Across Oceans and Against All Odds: My Journey to Freedom and Legacy

Marta Piechnik

Marta Piechnik is a highly accomplished real estate investor and construction company owner with a passion for helping others achieve financial freedom. With a proven track record in rentals, flips, wholesales, and Airbnb properties, she has mastered the art of scaling quickly and maximizing returns.

Renowned for her rapid success and commitment to empowering others, Marta leverages her expertise to mentor aspiring investors, guiding them toward financial independence through strategic real estate investments.

Instagram: @marta_piechnik

Facebook: Marta Piechnik

www.MartaPiechnik.com

At twelve years old, my life changed forever. My parents spoke the words I never expected to hear: "We're moving to America." For most, America symbolized endless opportunities and dreams come true. For me, a young girl leaving behind everything I had ever known in Poland, it felt like stepping into the unknown—both thrilling and terrifying at the same time.

But my American dream didn't begin there. It had started years earlier, shaped by heartbreak and sacrifice.

When I was five, my father left Poland for America with one mission: to create a better future for us. My mother would hold back tears as she explained why he couldn't come home. Years later, when I was nine, my mother also left, bringing my youngest sister for eye surgery. "We'll be back soon," she promised. But "soon" stretched into three and a half years. My brother and I stayed behind in Poland, waiting and wondering if our family would ever be whole again.

Poland, still recovering from communism, was a difficult place to grow up. Money was tight, opportunities were scarce, and even basic necessities felt like luxuries. Then, one day, everything changed. My parents returned, this time to take us with them to America.

I'll never forget the moment our plane landed in Chicago. The city stretched out before me, its towering buildings glittering in the distance. My heart raced as I thought, *This is it, the land where dreams come true.*

Reality, however, was different. We moved into a small apartment on Chicago's North Side. My father worked tirelessly running his small construction business, my mother cared for us at home, and I struggled to adjust to school—a confusing blur of unfamiliar faces and a language I didn't yet speak.

Despite the challenges, I adapted, working tirelessly to honor my family's sacrifices and build a better future. But just as I found my footing, life threw me another curveball. At 18, I was struck by a mysterious illness. My weight plummeted, and I could barely move. For months, I was bedridden, staring at the ceiling and wondering if I'd ever feel normal again.

But I refused to accept defeat. With determination and the right medical care, I fought my way back. That battle taught me one of life's most valuable lessons: no matter how dark things get, there is always a way forward.

After recovering, I threw myself into education, earning a business degree from DePaul University. Around this time, I began helping my father with his construction business. I still remember the first time I stepped onto a construction site. The air smelled of fresh concrete and sawdust, and the steady hum of activity filled the space—workers pouring foundations, machinery beeping, tools clinking. I loved every second of it. Watching an empty lot transform into a towering building gave me an immense sense of pride. I knew this industry was where I belonged.

But not everyone saw me that way.

As a 20-year-old woman in a male-dominated field, I faced constant doubt. On job sites, I was often mistaken for someone's assistant—or worse, someone's kid. I had to prove myself over and over, working longer hours and pushing harder than anyone else. Slowly, I earned respect. My attention to detail, ability to handle high-pressure situations, and drive to deliver projects on time and on budget became my trademarks. I wasn't just helping with the family business; I was helping to transform it into one of the largest masonry companies in Chicago.

Just when it seemed like everything was falling into place, the 2008 mortgage crisis hit.

The phone calls stopped. Projects were canceled. Overnight, we lost nearly two million dollars in unpaid invoices. I remember sitting at my desk, staring at piles of bills, wondering if we'd ever recover. But giving up was never an option. We regrouped, refocused, and shifted to public-sector projects to stay afloat.

Still, a question nagged at me: Is this all there is?

It was my husband who planted the seed of change. He handed me the book *Rich Dad Poor Dad* and said, "You need to read this." That book shifted my perspective. For the first time, I saw a path to true freedom: passive income. I didn't want to chase contracts forever. I wanted to build something lasting—a legacy.

In 2019, I took a leap into real estate investing, marking a pivotal shift in my career. My first property was nerve-wracking, but I quickly learned the ropes and scaled up. By the end of that year, I owned 25 properties. For the first time, I felt free. I was no longer tied to the grind of construction contracts. Instead, I was creating something lasting—a legacy for my growing family.

And my kids? They're the best part of my story.

Being a mother to three amazing children has inspired me in countless ways. I've made it my mission to teach them the power of financial independence and the freedom to live life on their own terms—and they've truly taken it to heart. Hand them a dollar, and they'll say, "Mom, can you invest this for me?" Watching their excitement and curiosity about real estate has been one of the greatest joys of my journey.

My oldest son has achieved remarkable success by embracing these teachings, and from a young age, my kids have shared their knowledge with classmates and even teachers, explaining how to invest in real estate. But they teach me just as much as I teach them. From introducing me to new AI tools and showing me how to effectively use platforms to helping me streamline property searches, they inspire me to stay sharp and innovative.

They also motivate me every single day to be better, to dream bigger, and to believe that I can achieve anything I set my mind to. Most importantly, they serve as an example to their peers and other families, proving that success doesn't have to mean climbing the corporate ladder or working to fulfill someone else's dreams.

My children remind me daily that the American Dream is no longer just about hard work—it's about innovation, adaptability, and creating your own path. It no longer requires a college degree to achieve success—it requires creativity, independence, and the courage to carve your own path.

Today, I spend my days transforming run-down properties into homes for families to enjoy. I've built a life where I can show up for my children. My career is no longer just about income—it's about empowerment. I mentor others, helping them break free from the nine-to-five grind and showing them that, with resilience and an open mind, they can achieve success beyond their wildest dreams.

Every challenge—every move across the world, every illness, every financial setback—has led me here. I've built a life of freedom, one where I no longer live by anyone else's rules. My mission now is to help others achieve the same independence and create legacies of their own.

From a little girl in Poland to a real estate entrepreneur in America, my journey is a testament to resilience, hope, and the belief that the only limits are the ones we place on ourselves.

Brick by Brick

Ewelina Rafael

Ewelina Rafael is a survivor, entrepreneur, and award-winning real estate professional who has built success from struggle. Born in post-communist Poland, she learned early that survival wasn't a choice—it was a necessity. Separated from her parents at five and stranded in a foreign country, she forged resilience in the face of hardship.

By 19, she was a single mother defying expectations, earning a double bachelor's degree from UIC while balancing school, work, and parenthood. She later spent a decade in public service with the Office of Adjudication and Review. In 2017, life tested her again, leaving her homeless with a child to support. Instead of breaking, she bet on herself, stepping into real estate with nothing but determination.

Today, she is a recognized leader in the industry, serving as past president of the Women's Council of Realtors Fox Valley, a Global Luxury Certified Agent, and the #1 Realtor on Social Media in Illinois (2022.) She has proven that home isn't found—it's built.

Ewelina lives in Chicago's suburbs with her partner, Dan, her daughters, Gianna (25) and Natalia (18), four cats, and a spirited shih tzu named Teddy.

As a co-author of *Slaying Chicago*, she shares her remarkable journey of survival and reinvention, proving that the greatest victories are the ones we create for ourselves.

Instagram: https://www.instragram.com/homesinillinois/
Facebook: https://www.facebook.com/ewelina.rafael/
Facebook: https://www.facebook.com/chicagorealtor13/
LinkedIn: https://www.linkedin.com/ewelina-rafael-3795866

The wail of the train whistle split the air, slicing through the bitter morning like a cruel farewell. It was not just a sound—it was a verdict, an irreversible moment that would separate me from everything I knew. My small hands trembled as I clutched the icy metal railing, my breath ragged and shallow, white puffs vanishing into the cold. The platform was alive—hurried footsteps, muffled voices, the distant cry of a baby—but for me, the world had shrunk to a single, shattering truth: my mother was leaving, and I could do nothing to stop it.

The rhythmic clanking of the train on the tracks swallowed everything else, its mechanical pulse drowning out my own ragged breaths, the rush of voices, the weight of goodbye hanging in the air. I wanted time to stop, for the train to freeze, for someone—anyone—to step in and say that this wasn't happening. But the world didn't bend to the desperation of a child.

I turned my head toward the train window, my eyes locking onto my mother's face. Pale, tear-streaked, pressed against the cold glass, her hands raised in a desperate, silent wave. A plea. A promise. A goodbye.

"Mama!" I screamed, my voice cracking with panic, my feet pounding against the frozen platform as I ran, chasing the train, chasing her. The metal wheels screeched, grinding against the tracks, and I ran harder, my breath burning my throat, my legs aching with the effort. She was still there, still watching me, her fingers splayed against the window as if she could reach through the glass and pull me to her.

And then, she was gone.

Steam billowed in thick clouds, swallowing her silhouette. The train surged forward, faster now, wheels spinning, distance growing. I ran until my legs gave out, collapsing onto the icy ground as the last trace of her disappeared into the horizon. The silence that followed was suffocating, vast and empty, pressing in from all sides.

I was five years old, and I had just learned my first real lesson about love: sometimes, love means leaving. And sometimes, love means pain.

I grew up in post-communist Poland, where endurance wasn't a choice—it was a necessity. Every day was a delicate balancing act between scarcity and survival, where ration books determined our meals and the length of the food lines dictated whether we would eat that day or go to bed hungry. I learned to wait, not because I wanted to, but because waiting was survival. I learned patience from hunger, resilience from uncertainty.

I watched my parents fight against a system designed to keep them in place. They refused to accept the life they were given. They dreamed beyond government rations, beyond endless lines, beyond the grey, crumbling buildings that threatened to box us in. They whispered of possibilities—a life where choices weren't dictated by the state, where opportunity wasn't a privilege for the few.

That hope led them to apply through Caritas, a nonprofit sponsoring refugees to the United States. But hope was slow-moving. While they waited for an answer that could change everything, my father left for Wiesbaden, Germany, taking whatever work he could find. He became a shadow in our lives—his presence marked only by the carefully wrapped packages that arrived from across the border.

Inside, there were chocolates, fruit, sometimes a small toy. But these packages were more than gifts. They were proof. Proof that he was still fighting for us. Proof that he had not forgotten. Proof that one day, we, too, would break free from the life we had been given.

For a while, it was just my mother and me in our cramped three-room apartment, a space we shared with my grandmother. The walls were tight, but somehow, they held love within them. Cousins, aunts, uncles—they came often, their laughter spilling through the kitchen, mingling with the scent of boiled potatoes and fresh bread. We were tangled in a shared pursuit of survival, bound together by the weight of what we lacked, but also by the warmth of what we still had: each other.

But love, as I would learn, does not soften the edges of separation. It does not make absence feel any less empty. And survival often demands sacrifice.

Then, the day arrived when my mother left to join my father in Germany. That moment didn't just change my life—it splintered it. I watched her pack the small, worn suitcase, folding clothes with hands that trembled, her face a mix of quiet determination and hidden sorrow. She told me she was going ahead to build the foundation for our future. But what does a child know of foundations, of futures? All I knew was the ache of her absence before she had even stepped out the door.

I was too young to understand that sacrifice often comes wrapped in heartbreak.

I stayed behind in Poland with my Aunt Grace, clinging to the fragile promise of a reunion while learning to live with the ache of absence. Every day felt stretched, time moving too slowly in a house that wasn't truly mine. I was surrounded by family, yet the absence of my parents left an emptiness that no amount of familiarity could fill. I listened for their voices in my sleep. I waited for letters with my name on them, fingers tracing the ink as if the words could bring them closer.

Even at such a young age, I understood something that would take years to fully articulate: home wasn't just a physical place—it was the people who made you feel safe. The loneliness settled deep within me, shaping my understanding of what it meant to be uprooted time and time again. The uncertainty of that time left an imprint, reminding me that home and stability were fragile, never guaranteed.

Days blurred into months, and what felt like an eternity was, in reality, a year. Then, finally, the letter arrived: our visas were approved. It was time. I was going to be with my parents again. My mother's arms, my father's voice, our family together—this was the moment I had been waiting for. I let myself believe that the waiting was over.

But fate had another cruel twist waiting for me.

When I arrived in Germany, my parents were already gone. Bureaucracy had intervened at the last moment—there was an issue with my visa. I could not fly with them. While they soared toward their new beginning, I was left standing in a foreign land at just five years old. Alone.

I was supposed to go to a host family, but when I arrived, they refused to take me. I was unwanted before I even stepped through the door. I had no home, no familiar faces, no comforting arms to hold me. I was handed off to a foster family—a Polish businessman and his German wife.

She was mostly kind, her warmth cautious, as if afraid to hold me too tightly. He was always gone, a shadow in the background, a man who existed in our house but never truly in my life. The walls of their home were unfamiliar, the language foreign, the customs strange. I felt like an intruder in my own existence.

I didn't speak their language, but they enrolled me in school, where I grasped at words like lifelines, clinging to anything that could anchor me in this unfamiliar place. Each day, I learned a little more—one new phrase, one new sentence—each word carving out a small space in a world that had not yet made room for me.

I was five years old, stranded between two worlds. I was not in Poland, but I was not in America. I belonged nowhere, floating in the in-between, waiting for a home that was always just beyond reach.

I spent two long years with my foster family before my visa situation was finally resolved. Two years of borrowed spaces, of learning to exist in a home that was not my own, of waking up every morning wondering when my real life would begin. Then, at last, in February 1988, I landed in Chicago.

My parents were waiting at the airport, their faces both familiar and distant, their arms open, their voices calling my name. Seeing them again was a collision of emotions—joy, relief, fear. I ran to them, but something inside me hesitated, as if part of me didn't fully believe they were real. Two years is a long time in the life of a child. Would they feel the same? Would I still fit into the family I had been forced to leave behind?

As they pulled me into their arms, I felt the weight of both longing and distance. I was big and small all at once—old enough to carry the scars of separation, young enough to still crave the safety of home. A child who had learned to survive without them, yet still aching for their presence. I had waited for this moment, but it was not the clean, happy ending I had imagined. It was something more complicated—a reunion stitched together with love and the unspoken weight of lost time.

But Chicago would teach me how to belong again.

It was both a haven and a battlefield—a place that tested me, but also transformed me. It was where I learned how to start over, how to navigate a world where I was both foreign and familiar. In the faces of other immigrants, I found pieces of my own story. We were bound by the same invisible thread—the cost of uprooting, the silent grief of leaving behind one life to build another.

We found solace in each other. We exchanged stories of struggle and survival, celebrated small victories—birthday parties, first days of school, a green card won after years of waiting. We were each other's safety net, proving that survival wasn't just about endurance—it was about lifting each other up.

In the hallways of my new school, I made friends who became family. People who understood me not just in words, but in shared experience. People whose stories mirrored my own, whose hands had also once trembled at an airport, whose hearts had also carried the weight of leaving and the hope of beginning again.

Chicago became home—not because it welcomed me with open arms, but because I fought to make it mine.

Then, another test arrived—one that would challenge not just my endurance, but my very sense of identity. At 18, I found myself pregnant with my oldest daughter, Gianna, while studying history and pre-law at university.

The weight of that reality hit me like a storm—sudden, relentless, and impossible to ignore. I was young, my entire future still unwritten, yet in an instant, I was responsible for another life. The world did not pause to let me catch my breath. Instead, the whispers came. People said my dreams were over, that I had derailed my future. That I had chosen struggle. That I would never finish school.

But I refused to let my story be written by someone else's expectations.

I fought harder. I balanced coursework with motherhood, exhaustion with determination. I learned how to function on stolen hours of sleep, how to quiet my own fears while soothing my newborn's cries. My days were an unrelenting cycle—early morning lectures, diaper changes between study sessions, late nights bent over textbooks while rocking Gianna to sleep.

I carried my books in one arm and my daughter in the other. I walked into classrooms with a baby on my hip, unashamed, unwilling to accept that motherhood and ambition could not coexist. There were moments when doubt crept in—when the weight of it all threatened to break me—but I pushed through, fueled by something greater than fear: the unwavering belief that I could build a future worthy of both of us.

Against all odds, I graduated with a double bachelor's degree from UIC, with Gianna at my side. She wasn't the end of my aspirations—she was my greatest motivation.

Every late night, every sacrifice, every tear shed was for her and the life we both deserved. I didn't just earn that degree for myself. I earned it for the little girl watching me, the one who would grow up knowing that strength is not about having an easy path—it's about refusing to give up, no matter how impossible the road ahead seems.

For ten years, I worked for the Office of Adjudication and Review, sitting in dimly lit courtrooms, listening to people at disability hearings, absorbing their stories of hardship, medical struggles, and perseverance. Their voices carried desperation, hope, frustration, resilience—sometimes all in the same breath.

I saw how the fight for stability—whether through health, finances, or a simple sense of belonging—was universal. The people before me had been displaced, forced to start over, to prove their worth in a system that often seemed stacked against them. Their stories were not so different from my own. I recognized the exhaustion in their eyes, the quiet pleading in their words, the unrelenting need to keep going despite the odds.

Day after day, I bore witness to their battles, their losses, and their triumphs. And yet, as I sat in that role, something inside me shifted. I wasn't content just listening to stories of survival—I wanted to write my own.

Then, in 2017, life unraveled again.

After a failed relationship, I found myself without a home, moving back into my parents' two-bedroom condo with my youngest daughter. Homelessness—once a fear I had outrun— had caught up to me again. At night, I lay awake, staring at the ceiling, wondering how I had ended up back where I started.

But I had already learned something far more valuable than fear: pain is temporary, and reinvention is always possible.

So, I bet on myself.

I walked away from the security of government work and stepped into the unknown world of real estate—an industry where I had no connections, no experience, just an unshakable determination to succeed.

The first few years were brutal. I spent long nights studying the market, building a brand, knocking on doors, hosting open houses where no one showed up. There were moments when doubt crept in, whispering that I had made a mistake, that I should go back to the safety of what I knew.

But I had never been one to back down.

I leaned into the skills I had spent years cultivating— understanding people, hearing their needs, advocating for them. Brick by brick, I built something from nothing.

And then, the work started to bear fruit.

I earned prestigious accolades, became president of the Women's Council of Realtors Fox Valley, earned my Global Luxury Certification, and was recognized as the #1 Realtor on Social Media in Illinois.

These weren't just titles—they were proof. Proof of the resilience I had cultivated through every trial, every setback, every moment when the world told me I couldn't.

Because I had been homeless. I had been doubted. I had been told I wouldn't make it.

And yet, I did.

More than the awards, the accolades, or the recognition, real estate gave me something far greater—it allowed me to create stability for others, something I had once so desperately sought for myself.

I have slayed Chicago—every obstacle, every setback, every doubt—and risen stronger, refusing to let my past dictate my future. I have walked through fire and emerged not just unscathed, but reforged. Now, I set my sights on Tampa—a new city, a new challenge, and another chance to carve meaning from the journey that brought me here.

The little girl who once stood on a frozen train platform, watching her world disappear, now stands at the threshold of homes, keys in hand, witnessing the joy of new beginnings. The same hands that once clutched the railing in despair now press open doors of possibility. The same feet that once ran after something slipping away now walk with purpose—leading others to the security I once craved.

This is my legacy.

Not just in real estate, but in resilience. Not just in sales, but in survival.

Every closing, every contract, every set of keys is more than a transaction—it is a testament to the battles I've fought, the nights I have endured, and the belief that home is never just a place.

It is something you create from the ground up.

Brick by brick.

Choice by choice.

Against all odds.

And now, I do for others what I once longed for myself.

I help them put down roots where they can grow, love, and dream.

I help them find the sense of belonging I once chased.

Because home was never something I stumbled upon.

It was something I built.

And now, I help others build theirs.

Small-Town Roots to Living Out

Big City Dreams

Holly Rust

Holly Rust, originally from Converse, Texas, and now a proud Chicagoan, is a professional content creator, social media branding expert, and small business coach. Her passion lies in empowering women entrepreneurs. She's a six-time author and her work has been featured in major publications and news sites, including *The Huffington Post*, *Good Housekeeping*, TODAY, MSN, Yahoo!, and more.

Her Chicago lifestyle brand has attracted partnerships with globally recognized brands such as Google, Broadway In Chicago, The Chicago Cubs, the NBA, and Hyundai, just to name a few. Her social media expertise and sales strategies have driven multimillion-dollar revenue for brands through affiliate programs as well.

Since 2023, Holly has developed multiple online masterclasses and eBooks to share her expertise with a global audience. To date, she has equipped over 60,000 students, reaching every continent, with the education needed to launch a business online, utilize automation tools, and implement digital marketing strategies.

Before becoming a digital entrepreneur, Holly was a director of sales and was an executive committee member for a luxury hotel in downtown Chicago. She spent a decade working in luxury hotels and, prior to that, worked in marketing for the NBA. Her most important roles are being a wife to Adam and a mom to Sebastian and Alexander.

Holly's rooted Southern charm, combined with her relentless ambition is why so many love working with her. She inspires them to dream big and equips them with the tools to turn those dreams into reality.

You can follow Holly @hollydays_chicago and read more at www.hollyrust.com

---

IT DOESN'T MATTER WHERE YOU START, IT MATTERS WHERE YOU FINISH.

"Holly, let me tell you something important, and I never want you to forget it. It doesn't matter where you start; it matters where you finish."

I was making a pit stop on my way to Chicago from San Antonio, with nothing but my clothes, my dog, Rocco, and a dream to start a new life, when my best friend's dad said these words to me. Over the last 20 years, those words have been my mantra, guiding me through every challenge and triumph—and this is my most coveted piece of advice. I still share it often today.

Now, let's hit rewind and go back to the very *start*, shall we?

My childhood was marked by uncertainty and instability. As the youngest of four kids with a father in the military, frequent moves and long stretches without him home became our reality. By fourth grade, I had already attended three different elementary schools, so making new friends only to say "goodbye" a few years later was extremely difficult for me. When we finally settled in Converse, Texas—the toll of this lifestyle was evident.

By junior high, my parents separated and eventually divorced, marking the start of a particularly difficult decade. Navigating this new life and rebuilding with my mother was eye-opening and, at times, emotionally debilitating. I handled it as many teens would: I kept myself extremely busy, I spent excessive amounts of time with my friends, and I ignored any feelings of sadness. Despite these struggles, my mom's resilience and determination to give me a normal life left a lasting impression. She worked night shifts because those paid more, but still managed to show up for all my games and other important events. She taught me to be independent, to always make my own money, and to just keep putting one foot in front of the other no matter what. I took all those tough life lessons to heart—and ran with them.

In college, the balancing act of paying my tuition (I didn't qualify for financial aid until I turned 23!), covering living expenses, juggling studies, working multiple jobs, and trying to enjoy a "normal" twentysomething life often felt crippling. With each passing hour, the dream of finishing school and building the life I envisioned seemed further out of reach. I went to school all morning, had an internship in the afternoon, and then I had a night shift waiting tables and bartending. It was a pretty common occurrence to see me behind the bar studying for an upcoming exam or getting my reading in for classes.

Fortunately, customers were always encouraging and often helped me with my homework.

By 25, I was buried in a mountain of debt and self-doubt about finishing school, but I made a promise to myself to finish what I started. I cut out distractions and shifted my mindset from self-pity to gratitude. I celebrated the small wins and any help I could get. I leaned on the support of a community and family who cheered me on. I was thankful I didn't turn to unhealthy coping mechanisms, which so many others I knew did. Most importantly, I embraced the belief that I—Holly—deserved success and happiness, too. Now, I just had to go out there to make it happen.

Despite countless setbacks, I stayed driven by the vision of a brighter future. Eight years after graduating high school, I finally earned my degree—with honors! I may have been (very) fashionably late to the party, but I still *showed up*. This milestone ignited a fire within me and proved that I was capable of doing HARD things.

With newfound confidence, I made a bold decision that would forever alter the course of my life shortly after graduation: I packed my bags, sold everything I owned, and moved 1,000 miles away to start fresh in Chicago. The city had fascinated me since childhood, thanks to iconic '80s movies like *Adventures in Babysitting* and *Ferris Bueller's Day Off*. When I arrived, I landed a job at a recently acquired hotel in the suburbs—though calling it a "hotel" would be generous. It was more of a "motel," and my role was to help turn it around. The main draw for me was that they offered free accommodations on the property until I could afford my own place. Let's just say this small-town Texas girl found herself a bit scared, especially given the questionable nightly activities that unfolded at this hotel (I'll spare you the details, but you can imagine). But hey, it was a free place to stay! Luckily, after just three months, I saved enough to move out. I stayed on staff at the hotel for a year and I did my job—we turned things around. That experience opened doors to opportunities I never could have anticipated.

Over the next decade, I climbed the corporate ladder in luxury hotels, earning multiple awards, incentive trips, and the respect of both peers and leaders in the industry. My relentless work ethic propelled me to a director of sales role, where I consistently exceeded multimillion-dollar goals and led a top-performing team. That hard work also secured me a coveted seat on the executive committee—a milestone I once thought was beyond reach. While on this committee, I learned from the best. I learned how to run a multimillion-dollar company. I learned how to budget and forecast. I learned how to sell and market in a sea of competition. Though I didn't realize it at the time, these lessons taught me the foundational skills of entrepreneurship.

In 2012, seeking a creative outlet, I started a lifestyle blog that would once again change the trajectory of my life. I poured my heart into creating relatable content about motherhood, food, style, and travel—topics that resonated deeply with my readers. Before long, major publications took notice, and my work was shared across platforms reaching millions. My blog was featured in a TODAY Show segment as one of the "funniest parents on Facebook" and I co-authored five parenting humor anthologies, one of which was an Amazon bestseller.

Although I was deeply invested in my growing hospitality career, something was missing. I longed for more time with my family and a greater sense of freedom. Hotels are a twenty-four/seven industry, and I found myself working more hours than I'd care to admit. As a result, I barely saw my husband and watched my two-year-old son grow up through the lens of daycare activity sheets. I knew a change was needed, and that change meant stepping away from my corporate role to finally pursue a dream I'd been nurturing for years: starting my own business in content creation and social media consulting. Resigning was terrifying. I had finally achieved the stability I had always desired, but deep down, I knew that if I had the courage to act, I had the strength to rebuild—again. Ironically, I made the decision to resign on the same day Pope Benedict XVI announced his resignation, the first and only pope to voluntarily step down. As a Catholic, I saw this as a sign—if he could do it, why couldn't I? It's a funny story, but if you're the kind of person who believes in signs like I am, you get it. The universe was sending me a message, and I took it. I cashed out my 401k, gave myself one year to make it happen, resigned, and got to work.

At first, I faced a lot of pushback from friends and colleagues. People didn't understand. They said social media was for kids, not businesses. They whispered behind my back. They told me I was "annoying" for posting so much, but I continued in my quest to prove them wrong. Well, we all know how that story turned out—today, social media marketing is often a business's lifeline to its success. The key takeaway is that I didn't need others to believe in my dream. It was *my* dream, and I believed in it.

Once I silenced the self-doubt and stopped worrying about what others thought, my media and consulting company began to skyrocket, and it hasn't slowed down since—twelve years later. Now those same people like to ask me how I did it.

I often have "pinch me" moments that bring me to tears. Ten-year-old Holly would be really proud. My story is a testament to the power of resilience, hard work, and the courage to take risks. I hope this serves as a reminder that no matter where you *start*, YOU have the power to write your own *finish line* story and create a life filled with purpose and possibility. Trust me, you are much stronger than you think you are.

One last thing before I go, I have to quote a favorite song from Panic! at the Disco because there were so many times I never thought I'd be able to say this, but here we are: "Hey look, Ma (and Pa) – I made it!"

A Love Letter to My Kind of Town...

Marilyn Santiago

Marilyn Santiago: A Beacon of Transformation and Inspiration. Known for her courage, creativity, and unshakeable optimism, Marilyn has shaped a remarkable career intertwining entrepreneurial excellence with community service. Transitioning from the media and entertainment industry, "Sunshine"—a nickname earned for her magnetic charisma and vibrant energy—has emerged as a leader in the construction and manufacturing industries.

Marilyn owns two successful companies. Sunshine Integrated Solutions leverages her expertise in branded content, promotional campaigns, and artist management to help clients forge strong connections with Hispanic audiences. Her second venture, Creative Architectural Resin Products (CARP), a manufacturing facility that produces exquisite resin-based faux architectural trims and accents for the construction industry. Made from high-density polymer resin, these products mimic the appearance and texture of natural materials, earning CARP a robust reputation and impressive growth in the architectural elements niche.

What truly distinguishes Marilyn is her unwavering passion and commitment to community service. Always caring for the underprivileged, Marilyn makes her influence noteworthy by serving on several notable boards at local and national levels. Her involvement leaves a lasting impact, consistently supporting and uplifting various organizations and making a difference to many.

Continuously evolving as an influential mentor, speaker, and communicator, Marilyn remains devoted to her faith, work, and life. "Sunshine" continues to illuminate and inspire all those around her.

Facebook/Instagram: @themarilynsantiago
themarilynsantiago@icloud.com

From Marilyn: I chose to share this without edits so it comes raw and unfiltered from my heart.

"Chicago has been very good to me."~ Sammy Sosa
"And to me too!" ~Marilyn Santiago

I wish I still lived in Chicago, thankfully, Chicago still lives in me!

I often reflect on the profound impact Chicago has had on my life, a city I consider my emotional support home. Though I was born and raised in Puerto Rico, the "Windy City" has woven itself into the very fabric of my being. Each day, I encounter what I call a "Chi-bite," a reminder of the city in the form of a call from a friend, a photo, or even an appetite for local cuisine. My beautiful Windy City has shaped me and taught me invaluable lessons, and for that, I am eternally grateful. I say with pride, Chicago made me a better person!

My love affair with the "City of Big Shoulders" started back in September, 1993, exactly two years after my mother passed away in Puerto Rico. Dark, very dark times for me. I landed at Midway carrying two large suitcases full of dreams, and a box full of a few art pieces. Some small paintings, a few sculptures, nothing spectacular or expensive, but very very meaningful to me. Those little art pieces were mementos of a life that almost got cut short. From that moment on, Chicago became my sanctuary, a place where hope blossomed amid the chaos.

My brother promised our mother on her deathbed that he would take me with him to Chicago and would not leave me on the island with my abusive husband. Back then I had been married for 3 years to whom I've thought was the love of my life, a disturbed man who himself turned out to have a past of abuse, abandonment and a drug addiction that averaged $2000 a day on intravenous heroin and crack cocaine.

I endured all kinds of pain and trauma, I was killed (yes, killed) several times, choked, hung, left for dead. I still live with broken bones, retinal detachment, cornea transplant and so on. Those were only the physical wounds...the mental, emotional, spiritual damage... let's say I'm still dealing with those. I remember the only way I could escape from my reality was going for a drive, taking Lake Shore Drive and letting the sights relax me. No matter the season, there was always beautiful scenery. Somehow, Chicago gave me hope, like no matter what the day brought me, there would come a better day!

My brother lived with his wife Mina and her children near the school where he was a bilingual teacher, on Chicago's South

Side. The neighborhood was a melting pot of humble, hardworking people from different backgrounds and cultures. Mexican, Black, Polish, and Puerto Rican communities. His school was near the heart of the Mexican community in Chicago, *"La Villita"* and where I learned one of my first Chicago lessons: Chicago gastronomy is spectacular! From street vendors to Michelin three-star marvels, Chicago has the best flavors for all kinds of palates! I remember tasting my first original tacos, Mexican, not Tex-Mex with cheddar ugh. I'm talking handmade corn tortillas, homemade refried beans, queso marca El Mexicano, diced onions, cilantro, and a drop of the hottest thing I've ever tasted, salsa! I also remember years later, my first time at Charlie Trotters, both extraordinary gastronomical experiences! Chicago's gastronomy has something for every palate! From street vendors to elegant dining, it became a celebration of my newfound life.

Back in those early days, job hunting was a daunting task. Long before the age of digital applications, there was no LinkedIn, no Indeed, not even Monster.com. It was just the classified sections, help wanted ads, good old physical resumes, printed in beautiful, fancy paper with cute, matching folders... so adorable! I applied to many, many positions—marketing, broadcasting, public relations, you name it.

I remember joking that my next step would be to climb to the rooftop of Willi's Tower (previously known as the Sears Tower) and drop hundreds of resumes from one of their antennas a la King Kong hehe. It was a tedious process, I had a good share of interviews. Yet no offers. Frustrating, but also inspiring! Such a great city, so advanced, so challenging. I knew I would get a great job, so I kept searching.

After a few weeks, I remember running low on cash and my hair color needed a touch-up. I had to get a job, no matter what. I had a hair emergency. It was then when Chicago taught me an important lesson about work. In Spanish, there's an adage that says *El Trabajo Es Honra* (Work is Honor). So I signed on to the

Daily Pay, for after a few days, I could have saved enough money to go to the salon on 63rd and Kedzie and get my hair done.

The first day on the Daily Pay, I wanted to die! Had to get up at 4 a.m. to get to the office, sign in and wait until some factory called for workers. Then the chosen group would hop on their minivan and drive to the factory, wherever they were. My first day was packing artificial putting green mats into their boxes. I broke my nails, my back was hurting, standing up for eight hours was no fun and this mean supervisor was bullying me for being a diva ugh. I remember telling her to take it easy it was my first day and I never did any factory work. She laughed at me and got me so angry that I told her to leave me alone, for I could be the boss of the boss of the boss of her boss to what she laughed at me and said "I don't care. Here, I am your boss and you do as I say." My blood still boils when I remember that moment.

I couldn't wait for the day to be over so that I could go back home and try to get a job in which I could use my qualifications. (Needless to say, they never called for me at the putting factory ha). My pay that day, after taxes, was $23. It took me a week to save enough money to get my hair done and I said after, "Never again." Thank God, never again and knock on wood! I learned to respect every person who has a job. I'll never forget that Work is Honor.

I realized that just sending resumes from help wanted ads in the newspapers would not cut it, so I started visiting all the Spanish language radio, TV stations, newspapers and ad agencies. No appointments, not a contact person. Just me and my fresh face asking for the general manager or president, ha! There were long waits sometimes, but I can say that I introduced myself to a large group of media executives in the city, some of which I still have on my speed dial! So the moment I started connecting with people, I started networking. I asked them about events and networkings that I could attend. I made connections with so many people, and that changed everything.

Mario Limon, General Manager of WTAQ, La Mexicana radio station, invited me to join the station's team at their table for a Puerto Rican celebration, where weeks later the keynote speaker became my first boss!

After my shortest interview ever, I got offered my first job as the press secretary of the Puerto Rico Federal Affairs Administration in Chicago. Since Puerto Rico is a commonwealth of the USA, this office was like the embassy of the island. I loved it! I had the privilege of accomplishing a lot while I worked there. It was a position where I could enact positive change within my community. It was perfect, because my boss was what they call in my Puerto Rico "una batata politica" or a "political potato" (an incompetent public employee who was hired due to political or personal influence). Whom as long as he took credit for all my accomplishments, he let me do lots of great things! I didn't care, people knew it was all me all along, haha!

During my tenure, I enhanced the quality of services for the Puerto Rican community. I produced the first Puerto Rican Film Festival, and together with whom up to this day is my best friend of all time, we produced the first (of many more) Hispanic Business Women's Conferences. I connected with so many people, made so many friends! Chicago gifted me some of the best friends ever. That Midwestern friendliness, you know how nice and friendly they (or we) can be. I also loved the fact that I had to work often in the Barrio by Logan Square, Humboldt Park, which are some of the trendiest, most beautiful places in the city!

This all sounds like a long time, but it was only like two months since I arrived; sadly, it didn't take long for my husband to escape rehab and fly to Chicago to find me.

My struggles were far from over. Just as I began to thrive professionally, he tracked me down, drawing me back into the turmoil I had hoped to escape. Yet, throughout the adversity, my Chicago family and friends emerged as pillars of strength. They rallied around me, helping me rediscover joy amidst the chaos. Hell officially followed me to the Windy City. It really was hell, but my "Chitown" never abandoned me.

Yes, Chicago never abandoned me.

My ex was a very disturbed person. He was evil with me, and while he was giving me most of the worst moments of my life, I was experiencing the most successful professional moments of my career. I received the support of my friends. From then on, I became an expert in working well under pressure. Thankfully, I kept evolving as a professional, getting better jobs every time. My next job, I became the executive director of a nonprofit organization that provided health education to the Hispanic community. We educated the public about HIV and AIDS and trained healthcare professionals about cultural sensitivity. It was a great opportunity to advocate, fundraise, and engage with another demographic. I felt so dismayed, so vulnerable... I learned to laugh while tearing up inside. Just like the old salsa song lyric, "*Pobre payaso, rie por no llorar*" (poor clown, laughs for not crying). I avoided my friends out of embarrassment, but they knew. Somehow, my friends found me and brought me back to life.

An opportunity in broadcasting came when Tiechnor Media (now Univision) decided to open a new Tropical Music radio station. They hired me as an on-air talent and in less than a month, I was promoted to program director of WLXX La X Tropical, probably my favorite job ever! We played the best tropical music, we produced quality programming, excellent promotions, we ran a tight operation. The station's ratings and sales were phenomenal. We started hosting and producing major events! Yet, with each professional milestone, I felt the grounding presence of Chicago cheering me on.

I don't know if it was the cold temperatures or the beauty of the city throughout its four seasons, but Chicago gave me strength to endure all the difficulties and challenges. Somehow I managed to excel as a professional while living a nightmare at home.

The connection I forged with this city was undeniable; its streets offered solace, its seasons reminded me of resilience. Chicago has been the backdrop to my story of survival, growth, and empowerment.

I departed from Chicago the same day my ex-husband was released from prison, vowing to return. Chicago isn't just a city; it is my emotional anchor, a testament to my journey, and a reminder of who I have become. I hold steadfast to the belief that I will come back and once again call this extraordinary place my home. It is here, among the skyscrapers and resilient souls, that I have learned to thrive. I'll be back... watch me!

Authenticity and Taking Bold Action

Monica Slivka

Embracing the road less traveled, Monica is a real estate professional and entrepreneur in Chicago, Ill. She is dedicated to creating connections and adding value authentically to those she interacts with daily. Monica has over a decade of experience in real estate investing, sales, and transforming distressed properties into beautiful welcoming spaces to call home. Formerly known as The Slivka Group, in 2024, Monica and her husband transitioned to The Danny Glick Group, a top Chicago real estate team with @properties Christie's International Real Estate Brokerage specializing in new development projects throughout Chicago. She has recently become more proactive in real estate sales as the previous five years were spent "behind the scenes" raising two toddlers and growing their community through Songs 'n Swings. Monica's drive for the business has been reinvigorated this past year as she welcomes new opportunities for 2025.

While real estate is her profession, her passion is fueled by building community. During the pandemic in 2020, she launched Songs 'n Swings, a program that brings indoor music and activity classes for children outdoors. Songs 'n Swings provides a welcoming environment for caregivers to bring their children to stay engaged. Blending both her profession and passion for cultivating community, Monica has taken the initiative, organizing neighborhood open house parties at Danny Glick Group's featured listings, creating memorable events for all involved while supporting local businesses.

In 2024, she founded My Turn, a purposeful empowering community for mamas. Events are tailored to help mamas leave their responsibilities at the door and take part in well-earned time for themselves. Events include networking, educational panels, play, self-care, health, wellness and more providing a supportive vibrant community for all who join including local business owners. Through these initiatives and growing communities, the possibilities are endless for what's to come.

Originally from Long Island, New York, Monica is a graduate of Florida Gulf Coast University in Southwest Florida where she and her husband met. (He was originally was from Chicago, so he brought her back north.) Following the footprints of several family members in the real estate trade, including her grandfather who established a successful real estate brokerage on Long Island, her stepmom who is in real estate and hospitality in Fort Myers Beach, Fla., and her sister's family focusing on the Tampa, Fla., market, Monica spent several years growing her real estate business in Fort Myers Beach prior to moving to Chicago. Her dad is to thank for her creativity. Currently residing in Edgewater, she and her husband have undertaken their most significant renovation project to date: a 1920s Chicago brick two-flat. Despite the challenges they faced, they transformed the house into a home, infusing their personal style into every recreated room. Monica is pursuing her interior design certification at the School of the Art Institute of Chicago (SAIC) to prepare for future projects.

Monica is a proud mama of two young children who continue to be the driving force behind her motivation to make a positive impact. She is a health and wellness enthusiast with a new love for pickleball. Her favorite time is spent on adventures outdoors with her family embracing their two energetic children during their youthful years, aiming to keep her family grounded and balanced.

Instagram: @monica_slivka

I was raised by a single, strong, and independent mother who was one of the first female mounted police officers in the NYPD (New York Police Department). She raised me on a farm in Long Island, and during my early childhood years, I realized my upbringing was unique. Each year, my classmates would take a field trip to our farm, where they could ride the ponies and play with the animals. My mom's "Pony Party" business was a huge success during summers, and though I was sometimes embarrassed to be surrounded by our "petting zoo" animals, I could see the pure joy and a big smile on her face as she entertained children on their pony rides. She had the best smile and absolutely loved being authentically herself while she created lifelong memories for these families. Unfortunately, my time with her was cut short due to mental illness, so as a young girl, I experienced a level of independence beyond that of most of my peers. But it is those cherished summers on the farm that I choose to remember, when her passion shone through. She was a trailblazer who added immense value to the lives of others.

Being so young, I was grateful to have supportive family members who welcomed me into their homes, treated me as their own, and guided me toward a brighter future. Authenticity entered my life, as a valuable lesson in resilience—the determination to keep moving forward, no matter how difficult the circumstance. As I grew older and learned to make my own choices, resilience continued to present itself time and time again. Embracing each challenge as an opportunity for growth, I continued on toward progress.

When I became pregnant with my daughter, I felt a deep calling to make a positive change for the next generation as I embraced motherhood. This compelled me to confront any limiting beliefs, expectations, past traumas, and strained relationships in life. As challenging as it was, doing the inner work allowed me to redefine my identity and purpose as a woman, wife, mother, family member, and friend. With authenticity's lesson on finding strength in vulnerability and forgiveness to move on with grace, I embarked on a journey of healing, layer by layer revealing the woman I had envisioned becoming. Fueled by inspiration for positive change, I was determined to build a wholesome home for our children to grow in confidence, feel safe, and take pride in their upbringing.

In mid-March 2020, I was a new mother to a beautiful four-month-old daughter, and my world—like everyone else's—was completely upended by the COVID-19 lockdown in Chicago. Grocery stores were overrun with frantic shoppers stocking up on essentials. Meanwhile, neighborhood playgrounds were closed, depriving children of crucial outlets for physical activity and engagement. My heart broke reading about children losing access to school meals and educational resources, which serve as vital safe havens for many. I feared the potential for increased domestic abuse, substance abuse, and mental health crises as families were confined at home without proper support. In that difficult moment, I knew I had to tap into my passion and purpose, so I created something authentic to support the children and parents who were navigating the profound impacts of the pandemic.

As a residential real estate professional with my husband Daniel, we connect with clients on a daily basis. Our role is to add value by introducing buyers and sellers and navigate transactions to closing. Even when the path does not exist, we strive to create opportunities to bridge the gaps from where clients are to where they want to be. This authentic, proactive approach to connecting and building relationships is at the core of what we do. When the pandemic hit, my role shifted to working behind the scenes—connecting with clients, handling marketing and website maintenance, and continuing to add value from a distance. This was a period of adapting and evolving so we could respond to our clients as a supportive resource through this challenging time. More so, it was an opportunity to be present with our daughter.

The in-person classes I had been taking Emma to had all closed down. This robbed me of a cherished opportunity to bond with my child. Not only did it impact my child's sensory learning, but as a new mom, I also suffered from a lack of community. Our only "outdoor" time was on walks, which we technically weren't even supposed to be taking. Daniel and I would find a field or walk by the lake, working out with our stroller beside us to keep our bodies moving during this time. As wonderful as the extra family time was, the isolation was not the life we had envisioned for ourselves as new parents in those first pandemic months. We realized we needed to take bold action—virtual classes just weren't keeping us engaged. We craved the positive, community environment of in-person events! In this moment, I knew we had to be proactive; we'd recognized a need and decided to do something about it. So in the summer of 2020, we launched Songs 'n Swings.

The fire in my heart while creating Songs 'n Swings was absolutely blazing! Of course, with that came a flood of doubts and a voice of fear to second-guess myself. "What if we get shut down during a class?" But authenticity called me back, urging me to hold on to my vision and push forward with a positive mental attitude. An "I CAN do it" attitude. Passion took the reins and fueled my dream of building something wonderful for our community—a warm, welcoming space where families can come together, engage, learn, and stay active while forming meaningful connections with other caregivers. At the time, I only knew a handful of families in Chicago with little ones, so I decided to take matters into my own hands. I whipped up a flyer and headed to the lake, excitedly inviting families I met along the way. Some were thrilled to hear about the event and couldn't wait to join in, while others were hesitant, worried about anything from germs to COVID-19. Those moments of rejection were tough, but they taught me the value of staying true to my purpose and not letting fear hold me back. I learned that in following my passion for Songs 'n Swings, something truly special would happen for all of us!

The night before our inaugural Songs 'n Swings music class in the park, we faced a little hiccup. Our musician called to share that he had a family emergency and couldn't make it. My heart raced as I thought about the eight families that had RSVP'd—I felt a mini panic attack rising! But just when I was starting to lose hope, he gave a recommendation for an experienced musician from a local music school who specialized in classes for children. Without hesitation, we secured his help for the class. The next morning, we laid out our blankets, greeted the five families who attended, and kicked off our very first Songs 'n Swings class. This was a reminder to trust the process and have faith that all will work out how it is meant to—a moment to embrace the unexpected and create a memorable experience for everyone involved!

Since that incredible day, we've hosted over 100 classes, creating opportunities for countless talented young musicians and supporting local business owners along the way. Our biggest events of the year include Halloween and end-of-year holiday parties, a summer bash, and local firehouse tours. I'm thrilled to share that our once-tiny guest list of just three people has blossomed into a vibrant community of more than 400! Throughout these past five years, we've proudly gathered donations for local charities, including Chicago food banks and shelters for women and children, and have established loyal partnerships with numerous sponsors. This support allows us to continue offering a variety of engaging activities and music classes complimentary for families. We even introduced fitness classes for new moms to attend with their babies and toddlers! With my husband and me as sponsors for many classes, our logo is branded on grocery tote bags, musical hand clappers, and bubble wands, and we even created a real estate coloring book illustrated by a talented friend. We have supported many of our Songs 'n Swings guests with their moves and welcomed their referrals in becoming a real estate resource. Never have I felt more aligned in the work that we do in building this community!

Parents often comment on how grateful they are for the friendships they've built through the Songs 'n Swings community, and the meaningful experiences they share with their little ones. It's heartwarming to see our children eagerly anticipate classes and how they want to be involved in welcoming our guests. They witness the joy in my smile during these classes, and more than anything, I hope that one day they will unleash their own passion, inspired by the purposeful community that we created together. What I cherish most about Songs 'n Swings is the overwhelming sense of gratitude that fills my heart and our community, reflecting our genuine spirit and authenticity!

Now a mom of two, I've recently channeled my creativity into launching My Turn, a vibrant purposeful community dedicated to mamas! My Turn is all about empowering mamas to come together, connect, and grow—no matter which stage of their parenting journey they are currently in. Events are focused on health and wellness, supporting local businesses, networking and of course having fun along the way with our pickleball meetups. Stay tuned for all the exciting developments ahead!

Authenticity is such a vital part of our daily lives, and its meaning can truly vary from person to person.

In my life, it has represented:

- Embracing being unique
- Resilience
- Honoring vulnerability and practicing forgiveness
- Creating value
- Adapting and evolving
- Discovering passion and purpose
- Taking bold actions and brave steps forward
- Maintaining a positive mental attitude
- Welcoming rejection as a learning experience
- Trusting the journey
- Gratitude

May this inspire you as you align with your own version of authenticity and take bold actions toward positive change, in writing the story of your life.

From Bee Stings to Badassery: How I Learned to Rewrite My Story (Without Waiting for Permission)

Tanya Smith

Tanya Smith is the fearless founder of Addelise, a branding and design studio that's all about turning bold ideas into powerful, purpose-driven brands. Her journey isn't just about success—it's about reinvention, resilience, and facing life's toughest challenges with a heart that won't quit.

Raised by a single mom, Tanya learned the importance of hard work early on, juggling jobs to put herself through college and graduating with honors. But life threw her a curveball in 2006, when tragedy struck with the sudden loss of her first husband, John, to a bee sting at just 27. In the depths of grief, Tanya discovered something profound—John's legacy lived on through his organ donations, saving seven lives. As she wheeled his heart to a waiting jet, a rainbow appeared in the sky, a sign she took as his message to keep moving forward.

This pivotal moment sparked a fire within Tanya to keep pushing, even when the road ahead seemed impossible. From that point on, she built an impressive career, becoming the only female VP of marketing and sales in a public sector company, growing it by fifty percent. But in 2016, inspired by her daughters and a new calling, Tanya left the corporate world to start Addelise—a studio dedicated to creating brands with purpose, passion, and a whole lot of heart.

Today, Addelise helps businesses big and small craft unforgettable brands, with clients featured in *Inc.*, *USA Today*, *Entrepreneur*, and *Forbes*. Tanya's story has become a beacon of hope for widowed women, proving that you can rebuild, reinvent, and rise—no matter what life throws your way.

Her mantra? "Chase your dreams, create boldly, and never underestimate the beauty of a rainbow after the storm." Because at the end of the day, your story is yours to write—and it's going to be one hell of a ride.

https://addelise.com/
https://www.instagram.com/addeliseinc/
https://www.facebook.com/addeliseinc
https://www.linkedin.com/in/addelise
http://awidows.world/

Writing this chapter has been unexpectedly difficult. It forced me to take a hard look inward, to sit with memories both beautiful and brutal. Life, for me, has felt like a relentless storm—wild, unpredictable, and sometimes downright cruel. If I laid all my truths bare, the story might read like a tragedy, full of loss, heartbreak, and moments that defy comprehension. But intertwined with those dark chapters are the brilliant, awe-inspiring days—the kind that shake you awake, remind you you're alive, and offer experiences that many may never know. My journey isn't a straight line; it's a winding road of resilience, reinvention, and refusing to let the storm define me.

I remember being a young girl, growing up on welfare with a single mom who worked tirelessly to create a life that felt full. And it was—full of love, of resilience, of doing whatever it took. But growing up fast was part of the deal. Helping raise my two younger sisters meant carrying a weight that most kids don't have to, a weight that molds you into someone people lean on. I became that person—the one who always steps up, who figures it out, who holds everything together. And I do love that about myself. But somewhere along the way, I learned to put everyone else first, tucking my own needs into the background like an afterthought. It's a hard habit to break—being strong, being reliable—until you realize that maybe, just maybe, it's okay to lean on yourself too.

All of that—every struggle, every responsibility, every lesson—engrained in me that I wanted more. I wanted a love that would stay, one that was real and true. I wanted a career I could map out, something that would give me stability if life ever decided to knock me sideways. I wanted my true love story to be about me first—about building a life I was proud of—while also sharing it with the person I would grow old with.

But life doesn't follow our carefully laid plans.

I met my best friend, the man I would marry, when I was 18. We built a life together for eight beautiful years. And then, just one year after we said, "I do," everything shattered. He was 27 when a single bee—or wasp—changed everything.

It plays in my mind like a movie now, in clips that don't always feel real. One moment, it was Labor Day weekend, and we were about to break ground on our dream home. The next, I was throwing dirt and a flower over my husband's casket. It felt unfair. I thought I did everything right. I worked hard. I loved deeply. I had plans. So why was he taken from me?

There are no words to describe the kind of grief that swallows you whole. I wasn't sure if I was even alive myself. I existed in a haze of pain, barely moving through the motions. But then, there was a moment—one that, even in the darkness, reminded me that love doesn't just disappear.

John was an organ donor, and his life saved seven others. As they prepared to harvest his organs, I went home to shower, trying to grasp the impossible reality I was living in. Hours later, I stood at the airport, wheeling my husband's heart—his precious heart—inside a Coleman cooler to a waiting jet. That heart was about to save a young man in New York City.

And then, just as the plane was preparing to leave, the most beautiful rainbow stretched across the sky.

It was John. I knew it was him. It was his way of telling me he was still with me. That moment didn't erase my pain, but it gave me something I so desperately needed: hope, even when I felt hopeless.

The days that followed John's passing were some of the darkest of my life. Grief is a beast that takes over, and for a while, I let it. I moved through life on autopilot, not really living—just existing. And then, one day, I literally fell down the stairs.

It was a wake-up call—one that felt less like an accident and more like God and John shaking me by the shoulders, saying, "Girl, wake up."

And so, I did.

I had already lost so much. Fear had nothing left to take from me. So instead of playing it safe, I leaned all the way in. I went after everything. I climbed the corporate ladder, becoming the only female VP of marketing and sales at a public sector company—where I grew the business significantly. But even that wasn't enough. I wanted more. I wanted to build something of my own.

Channeling your inner badass isn't always easy. Some days, she hides. But she's there, waiting to be unleashed.

I found mine in the wreckage. And now, I help others find theirs.

The days of grief shaped me, but they didn't define me. I eventually found love again and remarried, building a beautiful life with my husband, Dave. We have two incredible daughters, Addison and Elise, who brought me a whole new purpose. And let me tell you—nothing makes time feel more surreal than watching your five-year-old step onto the school bus while your three-year-old looks on.

That's when it hit me: What if I built something of my own?

I had spent years climbing the corporate ladder, becoming a VP, learning the ins and outs of business, branding, and marketing. But I had this creative fire in me—one I had pushed to the side for far too long. So, fresh off a conference, I drove back to the same beach I fled to after John died, on the ten-year anniversary of his passing. I cried as I drove, remembering that—just ten years earlier—I was so broken, but I had the courage to step into the unknown again. I walked into my house and told Dave, "I'm going to start my own branding and design company."

And just like that—Addelise was born.

In 2016, I walked away from the corporate world and founded Addelise—a branding and design studio dedicated to helping businesses build powerful, purpose-driven brands. I bootstrapped it from the ground up, fueled by passion, determination, and probably too much coffee. And now? We serve clients all over the United States, with ninety percent of our business coming from referrals. Companies we've worked with have been featured in *Inc., USA Today, Entrepreneur,* and *Forbes.*

But my success isn't just about business—it's about bold living. It's about proving that life after loss doesn't have to be small or safe. It's about showing other women—widows, entrepreneurs, dreamers—that they don't have to wait for permission to chase what sets their souls on fire.

Eight years in, I've bootstrapped and grown my business into something real—something that helps other businesses not just survive but thrive. At Addelise, we don't do cookie-cutter. We create brands that reflect the essence of the people behind them. Because at the end of the day, we're all our own personal brand—and confidence in that is everything.

I don't just run a marketing company. I'm a business-building bestie, a brand hype woman, and a firm believer that you don't have to play small. You can take risks. You can build something incredible. And you deserve to take up space.

Because life is too damn short for not taking a chance and choosing our own paths. Plus, we are saving one bad design at a time.

From Small Town to Beauty Empire

Kinga Szkotak

Kinga Szkotak is a licensed esthetician, lash educator, and business owner based in Chicago, Ill. Originally from Poland, Kinga's journey to success is a story of resilience, passion, and determination. From humble beginnings in a small town, she worked tirelessly to build her dream in the beauty industry, overcoming personal and professional obstacles along the way.

At the age of 18, she moved abroad, first to the UK and then to Norway, where she gained invaluable life experience. In 2017, she took a leap of faith and moved to the United States, where she pursued her passion for beauty while working as a dental assistant. Determined to create a better future, she enrolled in esthetician school and quickly made a name for herself in Chicago's competitive beauty industry.

Kinga is the founder of Look at Lash and the co-owner of Beauty Empire Salon and Spa Suites in Bartlett, Ill. As a lash educator, she is committed to empowering aspiring beauty professionals with knowledge and hands-on training. She specializes in eyelash extensions, lash lifts, and body sculpting, helping women feel confident and beautiful.

Kinga is always investing in new techniques and treatments to stay ahead in the industry. Her journey, shaped by perseverance and an unbreakable spirit, has inspired many to chase their dreams.

Her favorite quote, "Whatever you're not changing, you're choosing," reflects her philosophy on growth and success. Today, she continues to build her beauty empire, helping women enhance their confidence while sharing her expertise with the next generation of beauty professionals.

Instagram: @lash.body.face or @beauty.empire.bartlett

www.lookatlash.net

www.beautyempiresuites.com

Born in 1993 in a small Polish town with just 11,000 residents, my early years were far from a fairy tale. Growing up with two younger brothers, our lives took a devastating turn when my father, overwhelmed by responsibility, left us for another woman. Around the same time, I suffered another heartbreaking loss—my godfather, who was like a father to me, passed away at just 39 years old. His twin daughters were only two months old at the time. My world shattered into pieces.

My mother, now a single parent, faced unimaginable challenges to provide for us. There were days when we barely had enough to eat, often relying on essentials sent by my grandparents from the United States. Despite these struggles, I held onto dreams—just like any child would. My mother, the strongest woman I've ever known, worked tirelessly to support us. Surrounded by peers who had everything, we faced daily hardships. Winters were especially brutal. I still remember the struggle—our old windows let in freezing drafts, and my mother would seal the edges with blankets and tape to keep the cold out. We slept under two thick feather duvets. But no matter how hard things got, we always had each other.

At 18, driven by the need to help my family, I left Poland right after high school. I arrived in the UK with nothing but a suitcase and big dreams. I found a job at McDonald's, despite not speaking a word of English. My only responses were "OK" or "Yes," always paired with a nervous laugh to get by. The Polish community in the UK became my support system. Even though I worked grueling sixteen-hour shifts for minimum wage, I could barely afford a small rented room. My first room was with a couple I traveled with from Poland. It was a scary place—the door had only a simple key lock, the window had metal bars, and to get to the kitchen, you had to go down a basement staircase made entirely of bricks. Yes, you read that right—brick stairs leading into a basement kitchen.

After briefly returning to Poland and reuniting with an ex, I moved to Norway, where I lived for four years. At first, my job required a long commute—two trains, nearly an hour each way. I didn't speak Norwegian at all, but I was lucky to meet some great people. P. and M., two brothers, became like family to me, always there when I needed support. Eventually, I moved closer to my workplace, but the worst part was finishing late—around 10 p.m. The train stop was on a hill next to a dark forest, and there were no street lights at night. The speed at which I sprinted through that section of my route after work was insane!

Unfortunately, my relationship at the time was toxic, filled with jealousy and mistrust. We moved to the United States. I received my green card first, and thanks to my family's help, he was able to get his after me. I hoped things would change, but deep down, I knew they wouldn't. He was a good person, but we weren't right for each other. If someone constantly brings you down and isn't supportive, and you wake up with swollen eyes from crying every night, you have to find the courage to walk away—otherwise, you're wasting time with the wrong person.

A New Chapter in the United States

In 2017, I embarked on a new journey in the United States, chasing opportunities that once seemed unattainable. A friend recommended me for a job as a dental assistant, and I often wondered how different my life would have been if I had been born here. Maybe I would have pursued a career in dentistry. I loved both general and orthodontic dentistry. But deep down, my real passion had always been the beauty industry. In Poland, I had dreamed of working in beauty, but I never had the financial means to pursue it.

My ambition didn't stop at dentistry. Determined to elevate my life, I enrolled in esthetician school while juggling a demanding job. My hard work paid off in 2020 when I passed the Illinois state exam and started working at a beauty salon in Chicago. Within a year, I was renting my own space and building a loyal client base.

Starting a business in Chicago's competitive beauty industry wasn't easy. From securing funding and finding the right location to building a reliable clientele and managing daily operations, every step required courage, careful planning, and relentless determination. Interestingly, I always dreamed of living just ten minutes from work. Three months after renting my space, P. and I bought a house—just four minutes away!

Personal Growth and Finding True Support

Meeting P. was a turning point in my life. A former professional boxer with a disciplined routine, he became my rock, helping me grow personally and professionally. What once seemed impossible suddenly became achievable.

Within a week, I conquered my fear of driving on highways—a fear my ex had instilled in me by constantly telling me I wasn't capable. I got braces, started going to the gym, improved my diet, and lost nearly twenty pounds. Together, P. and I faced an even bigger challenge—infertility.

For five years, we tried everything—acupuncture, herbal remedies, detox supplements. One doctor tested my saliva for hormones and wrongly told me that my estrogen was too high and that I was at risk of developing cancer within ten years. I was put on hormonal pellets, which included testosterone and progesterone. I felt terrible.

I visited my gynecologist for a check-up and mentioned the pellets. He was shocked. "This treatment is for women going through menopause, not for someone trying to conceive," he told me. Tests later revealed I had cysts on both ovaries, which had grown by 2 cm within a year. Doctors recommended laparoscopic surgery and encouraged us to keep trying. Still, nothing changed.

We consulted four different gynecologists, all of whom recommended IVF. Time was slipping away, and we felt hopeless. I underwent endless blood tests—more than I had in my entire life. Every time, I'd receive a call saying something was wrong, only to redo the test and find out everything was actually fine. We were about to start fertility treatments when a client mentioned something called Mercier Therapy.

A Miracle and Building My Dream

Despite five gynecologists telling me I couldn't conceive naturally, Dr. Jennifer Mercier, the creator of Mercier Therapy, changed everything. Her technique, which involves abdominal massage to improve blood flow and uterine alignment, along with specific supplements, gave us new hope. She told me, "You need one year." After just six weeks of treatment—one session per week—I conceived on my first ovulation. Two months later, I was pregnant.

When I was expecting, P. decided it was time to buy our own commercial space so I could build my dream. Today, I proudly co-own Beauty Empire Salon and Spa Suites in Bartlett, Ill, and own Look at Lash. I'm a licensed esthetician, lash educator, and soon-to-be licensed massage therapist.

Lashes are the frame of a woman's face—their eyes start to smile! With body sculpting, I want women to feel confident and comfortable in their own skin. My dream has always been to create a beauty empire where every woman leaves feeling empowered—and now, I live that dream every day.

One book that profoundly shaped my mindset is *The Power of Your Subconscious Mind* by Joseph Murphy. It taught me that happiness is always within reach—it's a choice we make every moment.

My favorite quote is, "Whatever you're not changing, you're choosing." You have to break the cycle, move on, and find something that makes you happy. Looking back, I'm grateful for every obstacle—even those caused by my father. His mistakes helped shape me into the strong, resilient woman I am today.

About the Curator, Leigh M. Clark

Four-time best-selling author Leigh M. Clark is known for her inspiring books, including *The Dream is in Your Hands*, *Living Kindly*, and the *Slay the USA* series. Her work as an author has empowered and motivated countless readers by highlighting kindness, resilience, and the strength of community. In addition to her writing career, Leigh has over 20 years of experience as a business strategist, working with Fortune 500 companies to help them grow and succeed.

Leigh's latest project, the Slay the USA series, is a growing national movement that shines a spotlight on extraordinary women across the country who are leaving their mark on their communities and industries. Through this series, Leigh is empowering these women to share their stories of triumph, leadership, and impact, much like she has done in her own life. The series is rapidly expanding, highlighting women in cities from coast to coast, celebrating their contributions and inspiring others to follow their lead.

Leigh's expertise and passion for leadership and empowerment have made her a sought-after speaker, with multiple appearances on the TEDx stage. Her stories of kindness and personal growth have been featured in prominent publications like *HuffPost* and shared through appearances on *The Today Show* and the *Rachael Ray Show*.

As the founder of Kindleigh, a movement focused on giving back through acts of kindness, Leigh has led initiatives that have raised significant funds for charitable causes. Her mission is to create lasting change through kindness and sharing stories of impact, further solidifying her role as a leader in philanthropy.

Leigh resides in Southwest Florida with her son, Carter, and the love of her life. She's here to make an impact and leave her mark by illuminating others.

"Don't let the world change your heart. Let your heart change the world." - Leigh M. Clark

Instagram:@leighmclark @slaytheusa

www.leighmclark.com

www.slaytheusa.com

www.ingramcontent.com/pod-product-compliance
Lightning Source LLC
Chambersburg PA
CBHW061759120626
46550CB00005B/2059